'Poetry's many attributes include the capacity to abs
too deep to talk about. Its ability to be a creative and
life stages and ages is as limitless as your imagination. Pooky's timely, easy-to-read
and user-friendly book explores how the writing and reading of poetry can be a
valuable resource for communicating with the self and others.'

> – June Alexander, mental health advocate and author of
> *Using Writing as a Therapy for Eating Disorders*

'At last! A book that values and uses poetry as a therapeutic tool, as a way of
helping us make sense of ourselves. Unlike so many stereotypes about poetry,
this book is practical, unpretentious and heartfelt, with applications for helping
people – young and old – way beyond mental health settings. Pooky Knightsmith
has opened a very creative box for us to use.'

> – Nick Luxmoore, school counsellor and author of *Horny and Hormonal*,
> *Feeling Like Crap* and *Working with Anger and Young People*

'If you are "poetry-impaired" like me, Dr Knightsmith's book is a revelation.
Poetry is a language many of my depressed and suicidal adolescent clients speak
fluently, but one I have never had much confidence using in my therapy. This
beautiful, honest, and instructive book has given me another tool to use in
my work.'

> – Jonathan B. Singer, PhD Associate Professor, Loyola University, Chicago
> School of Social Work and co-author of *Suicide in Schools: A Practitioner's
> Guide to Multi-level Prevention, Assessment, Intervention, and Postvention*

'Whoever you are, whatever you do, here is a profoundly personal and moving
insight into the world of emotional and mental ill-health. But this book is much
more than that. Whilst many will identify with the dark depths of emotion
within her poems, Dr Knightsmith's greatest achievement is in offering teachers,
carers and friends not only a valuable resource to enable empathy, but also a
starting point to aid and encourage recovery.'

> – Dick Moore, Retired Head Teacher and Trainer
> for the Charlie Waller Memorial Trust

'This is a remarkable and original book. Pooky's poems, born out of her own
experience and that of those she has worked with, offer us real insight into the
complexities of living with and recovering from mental ill-health. The careful
structure of the book encourages exploration of relevant themes and is a welcome
addition to supporting recovery, when used within a therapeutic setting.'

> – Jessica Streeting MA, School Nurse and Advisor to Public
> Health England (www.schoolhealthstreet.co.uk)

by the same author

Self-Harm and Eating Disorders in Schools
A Guide to Whole-School Strategies and Practical Support
Pooky Knightsmith
Foreword by Sarah Brennan
ISBN 978 1 84905 584 0
eISBN 978 1 78450 031 3

of related interest

Poetry and Story Therapy
The Healing Power of Creative Expression
Geri Giebel Chavis
ISBN 978 1 84905 832 2
eISBN 978 0 85700 311 9

Cartooning Teen Stories
Using comics to explore key life issues with young people
Jenny Drew
ISBN 978 1 84905 631 1
eISBN 978 1 78450 106 8

Using Poetry to Promote Talking and Healing

Pooky Knightsmith

Foreword by Catherine Roche and Dr Fiona Pienaar

Jessica Kingsley *Publishers*
London and Philadelphia

First published in 2016
by Jessica Kingsley Publishers
73 Collier Street
London N1 9BE, UK
and
400 Market Street, Suite 400
Philadelphia, PA 19106, USA

www.jkp.com

Library of Congress Cataloging in Publication Data
Names: Knightsmith, Pooky.
Title: Using poetry to promote talking and healing / Pooky Knightsmith.
Description: London ; Philadelphia : Jessica Kingsley Publishers, 2016.
Identifiers: LCCN 2015049154 | ISBN 9781785920530
Subjects: LCSH: Poetry--Therapeutic use. | Psychotherapy.
Classification: LCC RC489.P6 K65 2016 | DDC 616.89/165--dc23
LC record available at http://lccn.loc.gov/2015049154

British Library Cataloguing in Publication Data
A CIP catalogue record for this book is available from the British Library

ISBN 978 1 78592 053 0
eISBN 978 1 78450 323 9

Printed and bound in Great Britain

For Tom, Joe and Mat
who have held my hand to Hell and back.

Contents

Foreword

Pooky Knightsmith's book *Using Poetry to Promote Talking and Healing*, is a resource that therapists will find extremely useful as a tool to support them in their facilitation of their clients' process. Clients, young and older, can find it challenging and sometimes impossible to even begin to verbalise their experiences, their thoughts, their feelings, their fears, their hopes. Often we need a creative means of helping them into the process. In Part One of Pooky's book she helpfully discusses how we might use poetry as a 'way in', as an instrument to aid reflection, to explore emotions, to consider 'what to do next', and to connect with others both emotionally and relationally. She also invites readers to consider how we can suggest that our clients write their own poetry as a therapeutic tool.

Part Two comprises an extensive collection of Pooky's own poetry, loosely organised into categories of potential presenting issues and mental health challenges. She opens this section with a helpful discussion on how to use her poetry in therapy, including reminding us that we should always keep the clients' wellbeing central to any decisions we make. We can envisage how her poems can be used as conversation starters or as a means to help a client explore an issue in more depth. The insight with which Pooky uses her poetry to write about stress, mental health and mental health challenges has the potential to provide clients, who may feel very isolated, with the understanding that they are not alone in their struggles.

In the final section, Part Three, Pooky provides insight and inspiration into how we can encourage clients to try their hand at writing poetry as a therapeutic process, or indeed experiment ourselves. As therapists we listen to our clients' stories and cannot help but be impacted, impressed, traumatised, emotionally affected in some way. We utilise personal therapy and clinical supervision to support us in our reflection and our understanding. Using Pooky's poetry to gain insight into our clients' journey's and writing our own as a reflective process - could be a valuable addition to our skills and practice, as a therapist.

Using Poetry to Promote Talking and Healing is a multi-faceted book that offers insight into the stress that we experience in our daily lives and the impact of mental health challenges. As such it is a resource that may deepen our ability to understand the issues clients bring to therapy or, indeed, that we are experiencing ourselves. In writing this book, Pooky has offered us insight into a wide range of poetic styles and given us an alternative creative approach to therapeutic processing.

Place2Be works therapeutically in schools with children, young people and parents. In our experience, and we have no doubt in the experience of the thousands of counsellors who have come through our organisation, creative approaches enable clients to explore otherwise challenging issues. Our challenges and problems are unique to each one of us and therapy facilitates a personal journey. After reviewing Pooky Knightsmith's anthology and guide we are of the opinion that *Using Poetry to Promote Talking and Healing* will provide therapists with a powerful 'common tool', accessible to all, yet with the potential to personalise each clients' journey.

Catherine Roche, CEO Place2Be
Dr Fiona Pienaar, Director of Clinical Services, Place2Be

Acknowledgements

Thank you to everyone who has taken the time to read, respond to and encourage my daily poetry writing. In particular, thank you to fellow poets Peter, Trish, Michael and Christine who've accompanied me on my poetic journey, and I on theirs.

This book has been written during a very difficult time for me – a time of complete mental breakdown. It would be wrong for those who have supported me to go unacknowledged here as this book somewhat charts my journey out of the deepest depths of anorexia and suicidality to a brighter place. The writing of it has been hugely therapeutic. There are too many people to thank individually – I've been overwhelmed by the support I've received, so thank you if you were among those who have reached out in some way. In particular, thank you to the triumvirate of men to whom this book is dedicated. Firstly to my husband Tom, the kindest, most supportive and most loyal friend I could hope for. Secondly to Joe who has gone to remarkable lengths to support me both as a friend and as a boss. Finally, to Mat my therapist, in whom I have finally found someone I can trust to help me heal the hurt.

Thank you too to Jane, the world's most inspiring English teacher who planted the first seeds of poetry in my brain back in secondary school and has helped to nurture both them and me in the intervening years. Finally, thank you to Jessica Kingsley Publishers to whom I made the world's worst pitch for this book by telling them I was sure they would not want to commission it… They disagreed, so my thanks to them for their faith in this project and my thanks to you for reading it and using the ideas herein to support those in your care. The work you do is invaluable.

Part One

Using poetry as a way in

Ideas, strategies and techniques

＊ ＊ ＊

Using poetry as a therapeutic tool
Sometimes it can be helpful to have a 'way in' to start discussions about difficult topics. Perhaps you are working with someone who has experienced trauma or who is travelling the long road to mental health recovery and you need a point of reference to start your conversations. Poetry can offer that. There are several ways you can use poetry to support your clients' difficult journeys – I've listed some in this part of the book to get you started and have included specific ideas with each poem shared in the anthology in Part Two to enable you to explore specific topics with someone in your care.

Poetry as a vehicle to discuss our feelings less directly
Poetry can be a great door opener during recovery discussions as it offers us the opportunity to talk about our feelings in the third person as we explore the feelings of the poet or the person the poem is about (I refer to this person as the 'subject' throughout this book). It often feels safer and easier to talk about someone else's experiences and feelings rather than our own, even if there are

many parallels. Any sentence that starts with 'I' is a tough one when we're talking about sensitive issues.

Ideas for exploring this:

- Ask the person in recovery to choose a poem that strikes a chord with them. Explore how the poem makes them feel. Ask questions about how they thought the poet might have felt when they wrote it.

- When considering a specific poem, come back to it more than once; does it evoke different feelings on different days? A poem which elicits fear and hopelessness on one day may inspire hope on another. Think about why this might be and how different people, with different issues and different frames of mind, might interpret the same poem in different ways at different times.

- Think about why the poet wrote the poem. What message were they trying to convey and who to?

- Talk about the person the poem is about. Think about what their life feels like each day – what would they find easy and hard, how might they feel at different times? What thoughts rush through their head as they lay down to sleep or as they wake up in the morning?

Poetry as a means for reflection

Poetry can be a powerful way of reflecting on how things were, how things are and how we'd like them to be. We can explore our hopes and fears through other people's poetry more safely than by looking into our own minds and lives.

Ideas for exploring this:

- Discuss why the poem was written – what was its aim and what might have inspired its writing?

- Think about how writing the poem made the poet feel.

- Consider the poem within a broader context; think about what might have happened before the snapshot captured in the poem as well as considering what might have happened next.

- When thinking about what happened next, explore the different ways that things could turn out depending on different choices and responses of people within the poem.

- Explore whether the person in the poem has the power to change the way things are – and if so, how.

- Consider the tone of the poem, is it sad, happy, hopeful, despairing? Consider how differently the same situation might have been portrayed if the poet had been in a different frame of mind that day.

Poetry as a means of exploring what we could do next

This can be especially helpful if you're working with a client in recovery who is not yet fully ready to embrace the recovery process and is ambivalent about the idea of change. You can explore 'what might happen next' through the eyes of the poet.

Ideas for exploring this:

- Talk about what you imagine might have happened later that day, the next day, next week, next year.

- Consider what changes or support would be needed to change the path that is currently being taken.

- Think about the positive and negative influences that could change the path that is taken after the poem.

- Think about how things will look for the person in the poem if nothing changes – how will things be next week or next year and how will they be feeling?

Poetry as a way to show someone how we're feeling

When we are in the grip of a mental or emotional wellbeing difficulty it can be hard to express just how we're feeling. We can feel helpless as people may want to help but don't know how to as they just don't understand. Or we can feel that people are unhelpful or hurtful unintentionally because they don't understand enough about our condition to know how to be supportive and kind. We can use poetry to explore some of these feelings and to consider different approaches which may, or may not, be helpful.

Ideas for exploring this:

- Ask your client to find a poem that touches upon some of their experiences or feelings. Read the poem and take a moment to just let it sit with you both.

- Discuss where the similarities and differences lie between a poem they've chosen and their own feelings.

- Cross out the parts of the poem that don't match how they're feeling so well and highlight the bits that are a really good fit – take a look at what you're left with and see if there's anything clearly missing. Could this form the basis for a new poem?

- Encourage your client to share a pertinent poem with people who care for them such as family or friends. Suggest that without offering an explanation first, they explore the thoughts of the person they've shown it to. How does it make them feel? What do they think is happening? How could they usefully help the person in the poem? What would be unhelpful?

Poetry as a reassurance that we are not alone in how we feel

We can often feel very alone and like we are the only person in the world who has ever experienced the difficulties we are currently facing. Reading a variety of poems about other people who've been in a similar situation to us can help us to feel less alone with our thoughts and feelings. It can help if we try to bring the person in the poem to life to make them feel more real.

Ideas for exploring this:

- Bring the person in the poem to life by doing a role play. If it feels comfortable to do so, the person in recovery takes on the role of the person suffering in the poem. Explore how they feel and what has led up to this moment and what their hopes for the future are.

- Switch roles, so the therapist/supporter takes on the role of the sufferer portrayed in the poem. Answer questions about how you think the sufferer might be feeling and actively encourage debate from the person in recovery if they think you're wrong or if they can add to what you've suggested.

- Give the person in the poem a name, a gender, a back story, a family – make them feel real and use them every now and then during therapy sessions by discussing how they might feel about things or why they might find certain situations difficult. This can be a useful distancing tool to use any time the person in recovery feels unable to express thoughts and feelings about themselves.

Writing poetry as part of recovery

As well as reading other people's poetry, we can, of course, write our own. Writing poetry can be a surprisingly powerful way of expressing our thoughts and feelings. We might write just for ourselves, or in order to share with others. The simple process of writing can be quite cathartic but once we feel comfortable sharing we often find that this is even more rewarding. This is explored in more depth in Part Three of this book but a few ideas to get you started are shared below.

Ideas for exploring this:

- If the person in recovery uses an especially poignant or relevant turn of phrase in your more general discussions, try to build it into a poem. You might take it as the title or first line, or you might simply incorporate the feeling it purveys within the poem.

- Take an existing poem and keep the lines that the person in recovery feels are most relevant to them and lose the rest. They could then write their own lines in to replace those that were less meaningful.

- Suggest the person in recovery adapts an existing poem that rhymes so that it no longer rhymes; think about how changing the rhyming structure impacts on the feelings that the poem stirs up. You can reverse this too by making a non-rhyming poem rhyme, though this is rather harder.

- They could write an additional verse or two for an existing poem, exploring what happens next. Alternatively, they could write an additional verse or two to precede the current poem which helps us to understand the potential back story.

- The person you are working with could write a poem about things that made them feel especially sad or angry. They could tear it up and discuss the feelings related to destroying it. Writing poetry that we intend to destroy can often help to free our imagination as we know that we are writing only for ourselves and our words will disappear soon.

Part Two

An anthology of poems for discussion

* * *

Here I share an anthology of my own poetry to use as starting points. Of course, you can use any poem that feels pertinent to the therapeutic situation and the ideas shared in Part One and in response to the poems in Part Two should act as guidance to help you use any poem as a starting point for discussion.

The poems are borne of my own experience, either as I battle with my own mental health or as I take on the experiences of others during my work in the field of mental health. My poems should be viewed as a starting point – they do not represent right or wrong, but merely the grounds for discussion. Some are painful, some may be considered triggering and some may contain points of view that you or your client disagree with. None of these things need present a problem with careful handling, but for these reasons, I would advise against using a poem in a therapeutic situation unless you have had a little time to read and consider it first and to think through some of the thoughts, feelings and experiences it may provoke during a discussion.

The poems in this section are loosely categorized, though you will see some overlap. Each poem is provided in full and is accompanied with suggested discussion starters and extension activities. All the poems in this section are downloadable. You can use these directly, or you can use them to inspire your own discussions and activities. If you would like to look beyond the poems shared here, there are many poetry websites and anthologies you could draw on. Or, of course, you may choose to write your own poems – or encourage your clients to do so. Some clients will be happy for you to share their poems anonymously with your other clients. This can prove very powerful for both the poet and the reader.

The rest of this section is devoted to sharing and exploring poems which are split by topic. The final topic explored is 'support'. Many of the poems in the 'support' section touch on topics listed earlier but I have split out the poems of support separately as they can be useful in a range of situations and can help us to begin to really understand what is and isn't helpful to our client in terms of support.

Abuse and bullying

— Same Lyrics, Different Song

Stop!
She said.
She said it loud,
But still she wasn't heard.
Could she have said it louder,
Or have used a different word?
If she had said it differently,
Or used a different tone,
Would he have said goodbye to her,
Or nicely walked her home?
She wasn't sure,
But what she knew,
Was something had gone wrong,
As if she sang some lyrics,
But he heard a different song.
And now it was too late to change,
To go back and undo,
Now her feelings overwhelmed her
And she knew not what to do.

Exploring this poem in a therapeutic setting

Questions

- What do you think happened?

- What did she expect to happen when she said 'Stop!'?

- What do you think she would expect to happen on another occasion if she said 'Stop'?

- What does the poet mean when she writes 'As if she sang some lyrics | But he heard a different song'?

- How do you think the subject of the poem feels?
- How do you think the person who didn't stop feels?
- Who do you imagine the poem to be about? What kind of people are they? What kind of relationship do the subjects of the poem have?
- Does the poem read differently if you switch the genders involved? Why?
- What do you think she did next?

Extension activities

- Imagine that a friend confided in you that this had happened to them. What would your advice be?
- Write a prose or poetry response to this poem, perhaps exploring what happens next or exploring the feelings involved.
- Explore whose responsibility it is to say stop and to physically stop in this situation. Consider it from both a legal and a moral point of view then explore what society expects, and consider whether this lines up with your discussion.

— Cyberbullied

As they teased her,
Poked,
And pointed,
Jeering from behind the safety
Of their computer screens,
She sat,
Silently crying.

Tears slowly worked their way down her face,
Their journey practiced and familiar.

Did they know how they hurt her?
She wondered.
Would they persist in this torture,
If they could see her tears?

It's easy, she thought, to be cruel,
When your computer shields you
From the pain you inflict.
But so hard to escape,
When you're the one it's aimed at.

Exploring this poem in a therapeutic setting

Questions

- Do you think that it feels different being cyberbullied than being bullied face to face? Why?
- How do you think the bullies would react if they could see the subject's face?
- Why does the subject find it so hard to escape from her bullies?
- What do you think the subject should do next?
- Would retaliating help in the short, medium or long term?
- Is there any way the subject could use the online world to help her?

Extension activities

- Write a poem from the point of view of the bullies
- Discuss what a typical day might look like for the subject – from the moment she wakes up to the moment she goes to sleep.
- Consider ways in which you could help a friend in this situation.
- Imagine you are with a group of friends who are poking fun at another friend online. They think it's a bit of harmless fun – how should you react? What might make that difficult to do?

Iron Gaze

His grip was like iron,
Though not a finger grazed her skin.
His gaze alone shackled her.
Each movement,
Each word,
…each thought,
Just for him.
What did he want to see?
How could she please him?
Or at least avoid his displeasure?
She hadn't known
That love could look this way.

Exploring this poem in a therapeutic setting

Questions

- 'Not a finger grazed her skin' – do you think that this makes the relationship any less or more abusive?

- What do you imagine the subject's friends and family thought about this relationship?

- Why do you suppose she feels 'shackled by his gaze'? How can a look make us feel helpless?

- What do you think she had expected from this relationship?

- What do you think she should do next?

Extension activities

- Write a letter to the subject, sharing your concerns as a friend and exploring what she might do next.

- Write a poem or some prose which precedes this poem and explores how this relationship started and how things changed over time.

- Write a list of your imagined pros and cons of this relationship.

The End, Maybe

He looked at her
With thinly veiled disgust.
She looked at him
With thinly veiled distrust.
What once worked
Was broken
And twisted and bent;
Where love
Was hatred
And time felt misspent.
She looked at him
And wished that she could leave.
He looked at her,
A look that could deceive.

Exploring this poem in a therapeutic setting

Questions

- Do you think her time really was misspent? Why?

- Do you think she would change things if she could?

- How do you suppose the relationship got to this point, how do you imagine it started?

- What do you think the poet means by the last lines 'He looked at her, | A look that could deceive'?

- Do you think she feels to blame for the turn this relationship has taken? Why?

Extension activities

- Change the feeling of this poem to reflect a positive relationship by replacing words throughout – consider which words you felt you needed to change and why.

- Consider the difference between love and hate and how love had turned to hatred here.

- Continue the poem to explore what you think the subject should do next.

Abused

After the storm,
She was lovely and sweet.
But kindness
And smiles
Should not be a treat.
Kindness and smiles
Are what we deserve,
Each day
From our parents,
That kindness preserves
The life living in us,
The joy in our souls,
But nastiness, bitterness
Slowly unfolds
The hate we did not know
Was hiding so deep,
The hatred that kindness
And love work to keep
From taking us over,
From ruling our lives,
But hatred creeps in
When we feel
We're despised
By the people
We love, and who
Should love us back;
The abuse of that love's
A most vicious attack.

Exploring this poem in a therapeutic setting

Questions

- What do you imagine the poet means by 'the storm'?
- How would the subject feel during a storm and why?
- What do you think the poem's subject expected of those around her?
- Do you think she felt responsible for the way she was treated? Should she feel responsible?
- Who could she look to for support, advice and guidance?

Extension activities

- Consider what a typical day would look like for the poem's subject – what parts of the day would be especially difficult and why?

- Consider the responsibilities of parents and their children. Think about how these are fulfilled, or not, for the people in this poem.

- Explore the feelings of the parent in the poem. How are they behaving and why? How do you think this makes them feel?

Frozen Out

She felt lonely,
And alone,
Even when the room was full.
No one wanted to utter her name
For fear of falling foul
Of The Bully.
The Bully had picked her,
Singled her out
As The Victim.
She was special
She supposed,
But she did not feel special.
She felt the pain of redirected eyes,
Ceased conversations,
Games cut short.
There was no beating,
And no biting,
But this was worse…
She felt alone
When surrounded by those
She once called her friends.

Exploring this poem in a therapeutic setting

Questions

- What do you imagine a typical day felt like for the subject of the poem?

- What does the poet mean by 'lonely and alone' – can we feel lonely when we are not alone?

- Is it relevant that the people freezing the subject out were once her friends?

- In what way is the subject 'special'? Should she be grateful to be special in this way?

- Why do you think this is happening?

- How does the bully feel?

Extension activities

- Consider different types of bullying and whether one type is more or less bad than another – and where their similarities lie.

- Write a feelings map for the subject of the poem. Consider how she feels at different points in the day and what can be done to relieve difficult feelings and promote positive ones.

- Write a letter from the subject to her bullies saying all the things she wishes she could say but feels too afraid to say aloud.

- Write a list of sources of support that the subject could turn to in this situation.

Walking Away

Afraid of what he'd see if he turned back,
He walked on.
His feet took him further and further
From his unspeakable crime.
His words had maimed and broken,
Bruising more heavily than the hardest punch.
On he walked.
A little less able to justify his actions
With each step forwards.
His pace increased
With his remorse.

Exploring this poem in a therapeutic setting

Questions

- What do you think happened?

- Why does 'his pace increase with his remorse'?

- Words are spoken of as if they have caused similar damage to physical abuse in this poem. What are your thoughts on that?

- Is remorse a helpful emotion here?

- What do you think happened just before and just after the point at which the poem takes place?

Extension activities

- Write a list of questions from the abused to their abuser.

- Consider what is more important – asking questions of the abuser or hearing the answers?

- Draw or paint how you think the abused and the abuser feel – you may choose to make your work abstract but you do not have to.

- Write the dialogue of a conversation between the abused and the abuser that provides some insight into what went wrong here.

— Betrayed

Did you ever hate someone
So much it hurt?
Wanted them gone from your life so badly,
That they filled your every waking thought?
Told yourself they were worthless,
Their point of view irrelevant
And misinformed,
Yet hung on their every word?
Found yourself seeking their approval
Though you know it cannot be won?
Waited for a sign they care,
That they cannot, will not give?
All this time, knowing their thoughts rarely turn to you.
That they can destroy your life
In an instant,
Without even trying.
That they truly do not care.
But you do.
You care so much
It hurts.

Exploring this poem in a therapeutic setting

Questions

- Who do you imagine is causing this hurt to the subject?

- What different form does this hurt take?

- Is emotional hurt more or less bad than physical hurt?

- How could the subject escape this pain?

- Why did the poet chose the title 'Betrayed'?

Extension activities

- Do you think the subject is safe right now? What steps could they take to keep themselves safe?

- How do you think the subject feels when they wake up in the morning? What things might worry them each day?

- Who could the subject talk to? How might this conversation go? Perhaps imagine this conversation with multiple different people and imagine how each would play out.

Anxiety and panic

— Anxiety

She says she's fine,
But her heart is pounding,
Ready to explode,
Her palms are sweating
And her breaths come short and shallow.
Right now the world is her enemy
And everything terrifies her.
She says she's fine
Because there's nothing else to say.
This is her normal now,
With each step,
Panic…

Exploring this poem in a therapeutic setting

Questions

- 'She says she's fine | Because there's nothing else to say.' Do you think this is true? Why?

- What is the subject of the poem feeling – how do you think they would describe what they are thinking and feeling?

- What could the subject of the poem do next to help themselves feel a little bit better?

- Why does the subject say she is fine even though everything terrifies her?

- What do you think other people would see and think if they looked at the girl in the poem?

Extension activities

- Write a list of potential panic triggers that could cause these kinds of feelings either for the poem's subject or for you. Consider how each of these might be managed or avoided.

- Put yourself in the position of a friend of the girl in the poem. What do you think you could do to help?

- Imagine what the next day would be like for the person in the poem – what would be better, worse or the same and what could she do to change this?

Feelings of Anxiety

Just because you do not share
My feelings of anxiety,
Doesn't mean those feelings
Are not there,
Should not be heard.

Just because you do not care
That I feel like I'm drowning,
Doesn't mean those feelings
Are my fault
Or well-deserved.

Just because you do not want
To help me fight these feelings,
Doesn't mean that everyone
Will always
Feel the same.

And just because you think that I
Should lie about these feelings
Does not mean that you are right
I will NOT
Feel ashamed.

Exploring this poem in a therapeutic setting

Questions

- What three words could you use to describe the sentiment of this poem?
- What kind of life to do you imagine the subject of this poem leads? What led you to paint that picture in your mind?
- What do you think the subject of this poem hopes for or dreams about?
- The subject promises 'I will NOT | Feel ashamed' – what are your thoughts on this?
- Who do you think the poem is written to? What do you think the relationship is like between the subject of the poem and the person it is written to?

Extension activities

- Rewrite the poem by changing the first line of each stanza to read 'Even if' rather than 'Just because' and alter the wording later in each stanza to offer a positive suggestion of how someone could help despite their feelings.

- What kind of music would suit the mood of this poem and why? Consider what track you think most represents the mood the poet portrays and listen to it with the poem in mind.

- Write an extra verse for this poem which explores any negative responses you have had to your own anxiety or similar issues.

Panic Rising

Anxiety bubbles up,
Threatening to overthrow me;
Panic like a stranglehold
Round my neck,
Clawing at my ribs,
Darting from my eyes,
Present in my jagged breaths,
All consuming.

I fumble for a life-saver,
Something to keep me buoyant
In turbulent waves of anxiety…
I fear I will drown today.

And then;
Music washes over me,
Deepening my breaths,
Slowing the beat of my heart,
Calming me,
Saving me from panic.
Today I will swim.

Exploring this poem in a therapeutic setting

Questions

- The poet explores panic in a very physical way – does this match your experience of panic? Can you describe how panic feels for you?

- What do you think of the poet's drown/swim analogy? Do you have days when you feel you will drown and days when you think you can swim?

- Music has a calming effect on the poet – does this work for you too?

- What strategies other than music might help someone calm when they're feeling panicked?

Extension activities

- Can you draw what panic feels like?

- Create a playlist which may help to calm you down at times of panic.

- Share your most calming song and talk through why you like it and how it makes you feel.

- Explore your body's physical response to listening to a calming song at a time when you are not feeling especially anxious. Think about the beat of your heart, the steadiness of your breathing, how strong and steady your arms and legs feel.

Stage Fright

Five hundred pairs of eyes watched him
As he took to the stage.
He walked, self-assured
Head held high,
Eyes looking to the sky.

When he spoke
Five hundred pairs of ears listened to him.
They heard
Every word,
They hung on every syllable.
Enraptured and engrossed.
He could not look more confident.
As he finished speaking
The applause was spontaneous,
Rapturous
And LOUD,
Drowned out only
By the sound of blood
Pumping in his ears.

As he masked his fears.
He thanked his audience,
Turned,
And purposefully
Strode from the stage,
And only then
Did he remove his mask.

Exploring this poem in a therapeutic setting

Questions

- How do you think the subject of the poem felt at different points in the poem?

- Why did the subject wear a mask?

- How do you think the audience members would feel if they were told how the subject was really feeling?

- Is it important to wear a mask? What happens if we choose not to put it on?

- What do you think the audience thought of the subject? Do you think the opinion of people backstage would differ significantly? If so, how?

Extension activities

- Write about a different situation in which someone might 'wear a mask' in order to hide their true feelings.

- Draw or describe the mask that we might wear to hide our true feelings.

- Consider how often masks are used in daily life – imagine who you might encounter in a typical day that might be wearing a mask and consider why they're wearing one.

— Panic Attack

Gripped with panic,
Heart beats fast.
Cannot manage,
'Till it's passed.
Can't control
The urge to cry.
Feel like
I'm going to die.
Breathing shallow,
Pounding head.
Skin is sallow,
Feet of lead.
Take control.
Take control.
Mustn't let the panic roll.
Holding tight
And breathing deep
Fear takes flight,
Calm feelings seep
Back into my
Weary mind
And shaking body.
I'm fine.
I'm fine.

Exploring this poem in a therapeutic setting

Questions

- What do you think might have triggered these feelings?
- How does the subject feel – what are the physical sensations? What are the accompanying emotions?
- What might help the panic to pass?
- Do you think other people can tell how the subject feels?
- How could a friend or passerby help? What would be unhelpful?
- Is there anything the subject could do to reduce the likelihood or impact of a future attack?

Extension activities

- How could you depict feelings of panic using shape or colour – can you draw or paint them?
- Do you think music could be a useful way of calming? Create a calming play list and talk about the songs you've chosen.
- Write a list of things that people who care about you could do to help you when you feel like this. Who could you usefully share it with?

— Scared

I am scared.
All the time.
With every breath,
And every step,
Fear accompanies me.
I am scared of the past.
I am scared of the future.
Most of all I am scared of now.
I am afraid of ending it all.
I am afraid of not ending it all.
I fear being a burden in life.
I fear being a burden in death.
Choices and decisions petrify me.
I fear the misdirection of others.
I don't trust my own choices.
The choices of others terrify me.
Fear accompanies me.
Constantly
And I can see no other way.
…and that scares me most of all.

Exploring this poem in a therapeutic setting

Questions

- Why do you think the subject is so afraid?

- The subject seems to feel afraid of all eventualities – 'I am afraid of ending it all. | I am afraid of not ending it all.' How do you think this feels?

- Does the subject's fear serve a purpose?

- Do you think the subject would prefer to feel less afraid?

- What steps could the subject take to feel less afraid?

Extension activities

- Write a diary entry for the poem's subject exploring the different triggers for fear in a typical day.

- Discuss an alternative way to end this poem which changes the sense of the whole poem.

- Write a poem or a few sentences in response to how the last line of this poem leaves you feeling.

Sleepless Nights

There's nowhere where I feel more alone,
Than tucked up in my bed in my sweet home,
Surrounded by my loving family,
With everyone asleep except for me.
I toss and turn but sleep eludes me still,
My problems could be solved with one small pill…
But no! I soldier on through sleepless nights,
Each night my restlessness reaching new heights.
I see you all lulled gently into sleep,
I watch you rest and inwardly I weep;
But sadness turns to laughter deep inside,
And as the night wears on my smile grows wide,
Because I know you're safe and well and sound.
My love for you's the best sleep pill I've found.

Exploring this poem in a therapeutic setting

Questions

- Is it really possible to feel alone whilst surrounded by other people? Can you think of a time when you've felt this way?

- Why do you suppose the subject chooses not to take sleeping pills to help with their sleeplessness?

- What sorts of things do you imagine the subject would think about whilst lying awake at night?

- How do you think the subject's family would feel if they were aware of these feelings?

- The subject seems to experience a whole range of emotions during the middle of the night – can you empathise with this?

Extension activities

- Write a list of ideas the subject could use to help improve sleep and manage sleepless nights.

- Imagine the subject asked one of their family members to write them a letter to be read in the middle of a lonely night – write the letter.

- Write a poem that explores your thoughts and feelings during the night.

Ruled by Anxiety

I can't get a thought in edgeways
When my head is full of fear,
Anxiety wreaks havoc
And my other thoughts aren't clear.
The part of me that's strong and sane
Is sitting in a well,
It tries to shout advice to me
I think, it's hard to tell
Because it sounds so distant
And its words are all obscured
By the nasty mumbo jumbo
That I'm trying to ignore.
Eventually I break and cave
And anxious thoughts run free.
And when they do,
For a short time
I wish I wasn't me.

Exploring this poem in a therapeutic setting

Questions

- It sounds like the subject has two opposing voices in their head – is that something you can identify with?

- Why does the subject say 'I wish I wasn't me' in the last line?

- What do you suppose makes the subject 'break and cave'?

- What does it feel like when 'anxious thoughts fun free'?

- What are the possible sources of the anxious thoughts the subject is experiencing?

Extension activities

- 'I can't get a thought in edgeways | When my head is full of fear' – use this as the starting point for your own poem.

- Write a list of ways that the subject could try to overcome the thoughts of fear filling their head.

- Discuss the pros and cons of the subject giving in to the fear in their head.

Loss and bereavement

— A New Hand to Hold

He stood and he stared
And then reached for the hand
Of the person he hoped
Would help him understand.
But the hand was not there,
And the bad feelings grew,
And before long he found
He knew not what to do.
The feelings grew bigger
And harder to tame,
They were ugly and scary,
He knew not their name.
He tried to contain them,
But when they burst out,
It changed him completely,
He'd scream and he'd shout.
But everyone thought
He was naughty and bad,
Nobody knew
That he'd just lost his Dad.
The hand that was missing
Unravelled his mind,
And made it too hard
To be calm and be kind.
Things got no better
For quite a long time,
Until one day a teacher said:
Why not hold mine?
Your Dad's hand is missing,
That must make you sad,
But if you hold my hand
We'll make things less bad.
So he reached out his fingers

With caution at first,
As he realised that things could not
Get any worse.
And as he held onto
This new hand, he found
That slowly, he put his feet
Back on the ground.
Things were not easy,
He had to work hard,
But he felt things improve
As he let down his guard.
And alongside his teacher
He felt safe and secure,
It felt better than feeling
So sad and unsure.

Exploring this poem in a therapeutic setting

Questions

- Why does the boy get angry?
- The poem talks about missing holding his Dad's hand – what do you think this represents? What else is missing now that the subject's Dad has gone?
- What do you think people think about the boy's bad behaviour?
- What do you think they would think if they knew he had lost his Dad?
- How could people help the boy to feel better?
- The boy feels sad and angry, is that okay?

Extension activities

- Write a poem or some prose that explores the thoughts of the boy as he starts to let his teacher hold his hand.
- What could different people do to support the boy? What could his family do? What could his teachers do? What could his friends do?
- What can the boy do to help himself?

— Before and After

Things changed the day
Her mother left,
Her Dad was always sad.
She tried to cheer her father up,
To make him feel less bad.
But tears kept rolling,
Tears on tears,
Each fat drop added
To her fears
That things would never be the same
As when her Mum was here.
As time passed by
Her father smiled,
And things seemed okay
For a while,
But deep inside
She knew for sure
That since her Mum
Walked out the door
That things would never
Be the same
As they had been
Before.

Exploring this poem in a therapeutic setting

Questions

- Will things ever be the same again?

- What will stay the same and what will change?

- Was it the subject's job to cheer her father up? Why? Why not?

- Who is cheering the subject up?

- How do you think the subject feels? What would help her?

Extension activities

- Write a poem about the things that will stay the same even though so much has changed.

- Consider the different reasons why the subject's Mum left and explore how the subject might feel about them.

- Write a diary entry for the subject the day before and the day after her Mum left.

Healing Hand

Each step was faltering.
She did not know how she could continue;
Alone.
So alone.
The loneliness a punch to the gut
Each time she recalled it.
She recalled it with each step.
As she walked
Her frame bowed and sagged,
The wind blown from her sails.
A small hand sought hers
And held her fingers tight,
Accompanying her death march
With a sprightly skip.
The change was almost imperceptible,
But with the next step,
She walked just a little taller.

Exploring this poem in a therapeutic setting

Questions

- Why does the subject feel so alone?
- 'A small hand sought hers | And held her fingers tight' – what did you envisage when you heard these lines? How else could it be interpreted?
- Why does the subject feel better when her hand is held?
- Do you think the subject walks taller because she really feels better or for another reason?
- Is it okay to struggle like the subject does or is it important to put on a brave face?

Extension activities

- Write a list of different things that might give us strength at a time like this.
- Write a poem from the perspective of a person holding the subject's hand – either physically or metaphorically.
- Imagine how the subject will feel in a year or five years. What will be different? What will be the same?

Leftover Love

Now that he was gone,
She wondered what to do
With the things left behind.
Trinkets,
Shoes,
Albums full of photographs
That nobody living recognised.
And her leftover love.

Exploring this poem in a therapeutic setting

Questions

- When you read the poem, what did you imagine had happened?
- How do you think the subject is feeling?
- What should she do with her leftover love?
- How will she feel if she does nothing?
- Who could she turn to for support?

Extension activities

- Write a poem that represents his side of the story.
- Write briefly about the concerns that different people might have for the subject – perhaps consider the point of view of a friend, a parent, a child, a doctor.
- Write a poem which explores how the subject managed her leftover love.

—— *Life Unbidden*

She stared ahead.
Unable or unwilling to comprehend.
It must be a mistake.
Dead?
Dead was so final.
She wanted,
Needed,
To believe he was sleeping,
His mind and body mending.
But deep down she knew
It would be
A long and dreamless sleep.
Meanwhile,
Her life,
A waking nightmare,
Went on,
Unbidden.

Exploring this poem in a therapeutic setting

Questions

- Life goes on. How do you think that makes the subject feel?

- How does it make you feel?

- When you read the poem, who did you imagine it was about? Why?

- Why does the subject crave the belief that their loved one is sleeping?

- It sounds as if the death was peaceful – do you think this will offer any solace to the subject?

Extension activities

- Re-read the poem imagining it is about somebody else (it could be about a child, a friend, a partner, a parent, a pet). How can different parts of the poem be interpreted differently?

- 'Her life, | A waking nightmare, | Went on, | Unbidden.' Imagine what this would look like day to day.

- Rewrite the end of the poem (from the word 'Meanwhile') and see how much you can change the tone of the poem.

— But You Died

The day you died,
I cried and cried.
It's been years now;
Still,
I cry inside.
In you,
I wish I could confide,
About this grief
I fail to hide.
But
You died.

Exploring this poem in a therapeutic setting

Questions

- Who do you think the poem is about?
- Why do you think the subject finds themselves thinking of their lost one today?
- What do you imagine they may want to confide?
- How do you think they are feeling today?
- How do you think they felt yesterday? How will they feel tomorrow?

Extension activities

- Write a poem to the subject from the lost one.
- Write the story behind the poem.
- Think about other people or places that the subject could confide in in the absence of their lost one. Consider the pros and cons of these alternatives.

— Nana's Wishes

As soon as I saw her, I knew she would die,
The sight of her old withered limbs made me cry,
She beckoned me over, put on a brave face,
She said she was ready, I thought it a lie.

Please do me a favour, get out of this place,
She said with the palm of her hand on my face,
It'll do you no good, it'll suck out your soul,
So walk out of here now, disappear without trace.

I heard what she said, though it sounded quite droll,
This place was a hungry and giant black hole,
The happiness went out of everyone there,
All of our life and our love this place stole.

I fed her some tea and I brushed her white hair,
And I checked she had toothpaste and clean underwear,
Then I gave her a kiss and with one knowing look,
I left her behind, and a part of me there.

I walked out forever, the courage it took,
To obey her strange wishes should not be mistook
For someone uncaring who just stayed away
So as she withered they'd not have to look.

I wanted to visit my Nana each day,
My heart said: Oh Nana don't send me away,
But she wanted me gone and she wanted me strong,
Because she knew soon that there would come a day.

When the grief of her passing would be our new song,
And she knew that it needed somebody quite strong,
To help all the others to handle their grief,
The day after I left, Nana sang her last song.

Exploring this poem in a therapeutic setting

Questions

- Why did Nana want the subject to leave?

- How do you think leaving made the subject feel?

- What do you think other people thought when the subject left?

- What do you think the subject thought other people thought of her leaving? – is this different to what they actually thought? Is that important?

- Do you think Nana was right to ask the subject to walk away?

Extension activities

- Imagine the conversation if the subject had refused Nana's wishes.
- Write or speak about how Nana is feeling at this time.
- Write a poem from the point of view of the subject when they heard that Nana had died.

Last Week's Flowers

Is there any sight more sad
Than last week's flowers?
Faces turned downwards,
Petals falling with the breeze
Of someone rushing past,
Their water slightly fetid.
It seems wrong to discard them
During their prime.
But sad to watch them
Pass their best
And bravely soldier on,
Trying to retain their glory.
But failing.
I worry
That this will be
My life also.

Exploring this poem in a therapeutic setting

Questions

- Is there any sight more sad than last week's flowers?

- What is sad about the sight of last week's flowers?

- How does this contrast with the sight and feeling of new flowers?

- What does the poet mean when she says 'I worry that this will be my life also'?

- How do you think the poet was feeling when they wrote this?

Extension activities

- Write a poem about giving or receiving fresh flowers.

- What questions would you like to ask the poet? Imagine how they might respond.

- In prose describe how last week's flowers might look – consider how this might translate to reflect our feelings.

— Is it Better to have loved and lost?

A moment lived
With love and hope,
Is worth a thousand more,
Where life is just
An aching hole,
When your love is no more.
The memories
Of good times passed,
Can live for months and years,
And in them we seek solace,
As we blink away the tears.
It's dangerous
To love too much,
We have so much to lose.
If those we love,
Leave us behind,
It's then for us to choose…
To dwell on loss,
And misery,
And wish we weren't apart.
Or think ourselves,
The lucky ones,
Who loved with all our heart.

Exploring this poem in a therapeutic setting

Questions

- Is it better to have loved and lost? Why?

- Is it dangerous to love too much? Why?

- What do you think is the poet's view on love – do you agree?

- How can we draw on memories of happier times to help ease our pain?

- If we have loved and lost, are we lucky as the poet suggests?

Extension activities

- Write a poem in response to this poem, which answers some of its questions and brings in your own point of view.

- Consider loss – if we have loved, even if a loved one leaves or dies, have we really lost?

- Consider the practical ways a friend might help when we lose a loved one. Think about how we can communicate these ideas and with whom.

Scars

Some wounds heal perfectly,
The edges neat and smooth,
The scar a small reminder
Of what happened long ago.
Some wounds heal less neatly,
Ragged edges don't quite match,
The lumps and bumps we live with
Like the pain not quite passed yet.
Some wounds will not heal at all,
They gape and ooze and weep,
Each day they bring us pain anew
Remorse, rage and regret.

Exploring this poem in a therapeutic setting

Questions

- What first came to mind when you read or heard this poem?
- This poem feels like it should rhyme, but it doesn't. Why do you think the poet made this choice?
- What is the poem about?
- Do you agree that some scars heal better than others?
- What can we do to help scars, of different types, to heal?

Extension activities

- Rewrite this poem so that it rhymes.
- Consider the scars in your own life – which category do they fall into and why?
- Think about whether you would prefer any of your scars to move to a different category – how might this be achieved?

Depression

The Tree Who Couldn't

It's summer, yet my leaves don't grow.
There is no leafy green on show.
There are no buds
That promise life,
No branches
Growing to the light.

I'm sitting dormant, sad and weak,
I look dark and dull and bleak.
At first you stop
To see what's wrong,
But that care ends
Before too long.

I sit, forgotten, in plain sight,
Amongst the trees whose boughs are bright
With blossoms, leaves
And birds who sing,
Whilst I stand bare,
A broken thing.

I wither, shying from the light,
I look more dull when days are bright.
The hot sun shines,
Reminding me
That I should grow,
Like other trees.

But sometimes it is hard to grow,
And put your leaves and flowers on show.
So I withdraw,
My branches bare,
Whilst brighter trees
Receive your care.

Exploring this poem in a therapeutic setting

Questions

- What is the poem about?
- Can you imagine the tree? How does it look?
- What feelings does this poem evoke for you?
- The poem alludes to bright days being harder than dull days – can you understand or identify with this?
- Do you think the analogy of the tree works? What might work better?

Extension activities

- Write a poem using a different analogy to tell a similar story.
- Draw, paint or describe the tree in the poem.
- Create a playlist that represents the different emotions explored in the poem. Consider why you've chosen each song and what it means to you.

— The Shadow

I see the shadow that follows you round,
That muffles your laughter,
Throws joy to the ground.
I see you attempt to escape its cold grip
But you cannot run fast enough,
Not long 'til you trip
And the shadow reclaims you,
It's icy and cold,
And it makes you feel lonely,
And worthless,
And old.
You pretend there's no shadow,
You don't say its name
But since its descent
You have not been the same.
I see the shadow
Because I've got one too,
But I'm far more practised at running
Than you…

Exploring this poem in a therapeutic setting

Questions

- What does the shadow represent?
- What is the point of this poem?
- Is it possible to outrun this kind of shadow?
- Is it easier to face shadows together or alone – why?
- 'You pretend there's no shadow, | You don't say its name' – what does this mean and why would someone act this way?

Extension activities

- The poet uses words that portray cold and darkness when talking about the shadow – what other words might fit?
- What words evoke the opposite thoughts and feelings of this poem?
- Create a poem using either one of the lists of words you've created.

— Dark

To those who do not know dark,
It looks always the same;
But those of us
Who are familiar,
(But not friendly)
With darkness know
That there are many, many shades.

There is the dark that comes quickly.
There is the dark that creeps.
There is the dark so dense you cannot see your hand before your face,
And the dark that is not so quite so dark,
Where there is a promise of light.

There is grey dark,
And blue dark,
Murky dark,
And vivid dark;
These different types of dark form an entire palette
To those
In the know.

To others,
Dark, is just
Dark.

Exploring this poem in a therapeutic setting

Questions

- Is dark just dark?
- Explore in a little more depth the types of dark that the poet describes.
- Can you think of any more types of dark not alluded to in the poem?
- Why are some people more aware of the many shades of dark?
- Do you think that once you have known many types of dark you will always remember them, even if you no longer experience them?

Extension activities

- Represent the different types of dark in colour or collage.
- Think of a piece of music that echoes the feelings of each of the types of dark you've explored. How does the music make you feel?
- Write a poem or a piece of prose from the point of view of someone trying to understand the different types of dark but who just doesn't get it.

Head Fight

The fight is only in my imagination
But it feels more real
Than reality.
More real than acrid words
And roughened hands
And spit
And bile
And hatred.
It feels more real
Than any fight I've ever had,
For I can exit those.
Sit on another plane,
Untouched by fists and words,
As cheeks and egos
Bruise and blister
Unfelt.
But this fight,
Which is only in my head,
Hurts so badly
I weep with pain…
And run.
From myself.

Exploring this poem in a therapeutic setting

Questions

- Does this sound familiar?

- Do you think it is harder to fight physical or mental battles? Why?

- What do you think the poet means when she says she runs from herself?

- Why does fighting mental battles hurt so much?

- What could the poet do to ease the pain of these battles?

Extension activities

- What questions would you like to ask the poet about this poem – how do you imagine she'd respond?

- What frame of mind do you think the poet is in? How might a loved one support her?

- Write a poem or piece of prose that uses the analogy of a physical fight to explore one of your mental battles (or one of someone else's if you prefer).

Numb

It was a numb day,
A day without feeling;
No panic,
No anxiety,
No sadness,
No joy.
The days without feeling
Were gifts from the darkness,
But she longed
For a day
Filled with hope.

Exploring this poem in a therapeutic setting

Questions

- Why did a numb day feel like a gift?
- Does the notion of a 'numb day' make sense to you – can you explain it?
- Do you think many people would understand the notion of a numb day – why/why not?
- If an otherwise healthy person experienced a 'numb day' out of nowhere, how do you think it would make them feel? How would they respond physically and emotionally?
- What might trigger the different types of days alluded to in the poem?

Extension activities

- Write a poem that depicts one of the different types of days the poet mentions.
- Rewrite this poem to create a rhyming poem – compare and contrast the two poems.
- Draw or paint a numb day.

Creeping Ivy

The ivy crept closer to the windows each year,
Working its way quietly over the house's façade,
Invading cracks and crevices
Leaving no brick uncovered.
Soon the windows would be obscured,
The door choked,
By the dark and poisoned ivy
That you never saw grow…

Exploring this poem in a therapeutic setting

Questions

- What do you think the ivy represents?
- In the last line who do you think 'You' refers to?
- Why is it hard to see it grow?
- How does this poem make you feel?
- Should the ivy be left to grow?

Extension activities

- Write a short story using the ivy analogy.
- Write a poem using an alternative analogy to the ivy.
- Find three words that you think give the poem power and meaning. Experiment with substituting these words – how does it change the feel or sense of the poem?

Rose Tinted

I have a pair of glasses,
And they make the world look good.
This special pair of glasses
Help me see the way I should.

But some days I misplace them,
Or forget to put them on,
And without my special glasses on,
I see the world all wrong.

Things go topsy turvy
And they all look dull and grey,
Even in bright light I'm shadowed,
Dark won't go away.

When I go without my glasses
Life is hard,
And I feel scared,
So each day I put my glasses on
Breathe deep,
Then I'm prepared.

Exploring this poem in a therapeutic setting

Questions

- What do the glasses represent?
- Does this sound familiar – do you have any routines that help you face the world on difficult days?
- Why are the glasses rose tinted – is this a good thing?
- 'This special pair of glasses | Help me see the way I should' – is there a right and a wrong way of seeing the world?
- Does everyone have to prepare themselves to face the world? Why/why not?

Extension activities

- Write a new poem using the first four lines of this poem as your starting point.
- Write a list of alternative items or techniques that could be used to help us prepare to face the world.
- Consider what props you use to help each day use manageable – explore which props are helpful and unhelpful and consider how you can get the most out of your useful props.

Matter over Mind

Mind over matter
Is easy to say,
But what if your mind
Doesn't feel the same way?
What if your mind
Is all crooked and bent,
And knocked out of shape,
And exhausted and spent?
What if your mind conspires
Darkly with you,
To ensure that you don't
Enjoy things that you do,
And to make them feel hard,
And to show you a way,
To make sure that tomorrow
Is not a new day?
For some of us life is more
Matter over mind,
Because
Our dark thoughts
Leave our outlook quite blind.

Exploring this poem in a therapeutic setting

Questions

- What do you think of the phrase 'mind over matter'?

- Why would your mind 'Conspire darkly with you'? What would this feel like and how might it play out in daily life?

- How can our mind take enjoyment out of the things that we do? What kind of things might be impacted?

- How do you think the poet feels being controlled, rather than controlling, her mind?

- Are any of us really in control of our minds? Is this a realistic aim?

Extension activities

- Recall times recently when you have felt more in control of your mind. Consider what made you more able to control your mind on these occasions and whether this might work again.

- Select five lines to remove from this poem. Replace them with your own words. How does this change the feel of the poem?

- Write a short dialogue between the poet and her mind – what does the poet want? What is her mind trying to do? What does the poet think her mind is trying to do? Are they enemies?

— And So She Drank

Disappointed,
She looked at her bounty.
Two cats, one fish,
A child that didn't love her,
And a husband, estranged.
Her time had been wasted.
The oxygen she breathed
Better spent on another,
And so she drank.
Oblivion, her only comfort.

Exploring this poem in a therapeutic setting

Questions

- Do you think the subject has made a realistic assessment of her lot in life?
- Why do you suppose she thinks her child doesn't love her?
- What comfort would come with oblivion?
- 'Her time had been wasted. | The oxygen she breathed | Better spent on another'. Why would the subject feel this way? Is she right?
- This poem is short. Do you think it says all it needs to? What is missing?

Extension activities

- Rewrite the poem to incorporate any missing elements you identified.
- 'Her time had been wasted. | The oxygen she breathed | Better spent on another' – imagine how different people in the subject's life would feel if they knew she was thinking this way. How might a friend, her child, a parent or her estranged husband respond?
- Rewrite this poem so that every line is a question. Consider these questions.

Highs and Lows

Life
Can feel
Hard to bear
And most unfair
An uphill struggle
And nightmarish muddle
You're fighting on your own.
But stop and look, and you will see
That though you're fully grown,
All around are helping hands,
Who'll guide and care and
Understand, as you find
Your way down. Let
Them help you,
Let them try
And never
Be afraid
To cry
X

Exploring this poem in a therapeutic setting

Questions

- Do you think the way this poem appears on the page adds to or detracts from its message? Why?

- How much difference does it make facing each day alone compared to letting people help us?

- Why are we hesitant to invite the help of others?

- The poem says we should never be afraid to cry – do you agree? Why/why not?

- Who do you imagine the poem is written to?

Extension activities

- Rewrite or rearrange this poem so that it appears differently on the page – how does this impact on your perception of the poem? How do the two poems compare?

- The poem says 'All around are helping hands'. Write a list of the helping hands you can think of – consider not only people you know but other sources of support too. For each of these think about when and how they might help and how you might feel asking for their support.

- Write a poem in response to this one by someone who is not ready to ask for help – use your poem to explore why they are so unsure. Consider how these concerns might be addressed.

Peaks and Ditches

Without life's downs,
There'd be no ups,
No light-hearted refrains;
With nothing to compare them to,
The ups would seem mundane.

Without the ups,
The downs would seem,
The way that things should be.
Glumly we'd accept the downs,
And not know differently.

So ups and downs we thank you,
Though we may not at the time,
We need you both, to help us find
Life's rhythm and life's rhyme.

Exploring this poem in a therapeutic setting

Questions

- Do you agree that we need downs to help us appreciate ups?

- Does life consist of a rhythm of ups and downs for most people?

- Can you think of anyone who seems only to have ups? Do you imagine there are any downs you don't know about?

- Have you had a time when it felt like life was only downs? Where might you find little ups to help you through?

- Do you think ups would really seem mundane without downs to compare them to?

Extension activities

- Identify a list of small pleasures and joys that could bring little ups during darker times.

- Write a poem that celebrates small pleasures in life

- Rewrite the last line of each verse – does your choice of line change the meaning or tone?

Good Days, Bad Days

Some days I long
To soar high
And fly free
Like an eagle,
I'd watch
The world
Far beneath me.

But some days I long
To stay
Closed up inside,
In a big padded box
From the World,
I would hide.

I can never be sure
What tomorrow will bring,
Will I crouch down and whisper
Or stand tall and sing?
Will I embrace the world
With a smile on my face,
Or keep myself hidden
Feeling like a disgrace?

I embrace the good days,
And battle the bad,
Because some days I'm happy
But some days I'm sad.

Exploring this poem in a therapeutic setting

Questions

- Can you identify with this?

- What makes some days happy and some days sad?

- Can sad days become happy days? How?

- How can we battle the bad days?

- How can we embrace the good days?

Extension activities

- Write about a good day and a bad day – compare and contrast them and try to understand what the key differences are.

- Write a list of ways of battling bad days.

- Consider a time a bad day became a good day – what went right? What could you learn from that day? Conversely, if a good day became a bad day recently, think what lessons you can learn from that day to try to avoid that happening again in the future.

— Don't Step into the Darkness

Have you ever stepped into the darkness,
To the place that isn't there,
To the place where all your worries are,
And everyone who cares
Feels distant and unloving,
And a little out of reach,
Trapped behind a barrier,
You very barely breach.

The darkness is consuming,
And it's not a happy place,
You want to leave,
You try to leave,
But in truth, you cannot face
The light shining on your problems,
For them to take up centre stage,
And so you suffer, silent
In the corner of your cage.

If you step into the darkness,
It can be hard to step back out,
In fact it's quite impossible
If you find you are without,
A lifeline or a loved one,
Who can help you find the way,
To the light, and hold your hand there,
Whilst the darkness fades to grey.

If you've not stepped into the darkness,
Please do try to stay away,
Cast about for lifelines
And search for another way.
It won't make things feel better,
It just makes them feel worse.
It's dark and cold and lonely,
And it feels like a curse.

Exploring this poem in a therapeutic setting

Questions

- What is 'the darkness' described in the poem?

- Can you describe the darkness in your own words?

- This poem suggests that we have a choice over whether to step into the darkness – do you think that's true?

- What are the potential 'lifelines' that the poet refers to?
- Do you agree with the sentiment of this poem, that the darkness seems inviting but is best avoided?

Extension activities

- Write a list of people or things that can act as lifelines to stop people entering the darkness or to help them find their way back out again.
- Write a poem by someone trapped into the darkness who finds their way out.
- Consider darkness and light and whether there is a place in between – describe it in prose or write a poem about it.

— Outwardly Smiling

You see a smile
And look away.
'She's not depressed.'
I hear you say.
'She's smiling, laughing, full of fun.'

Believe me,
I'm not the only one
Who's sad inside,
But brave of face,
Trying hard not to embrace
The Demons lurking just within,
Stretching, poking at my skin.

They want to make their presence known,
And make me feel quite alone,
With Demons as my company.
That mustn't happen.
Not to me.
So full of hate, despair and bile,
I'll wear my mask
And force a smile.

Exploring this poem in a therapeutic setting

Questions

- Can you be depressed and smiling?
- Why do people assume that if you smile, you're okay?
- Is it easy to pretend to be okay when you're not?
- Why does the poet 'force a smile?' Can you empathise with this?
- What are the 'Demons lurking just within, | Stretching, poking at my skin'?

Extension activities

- Write a poem or a piece of prose that describes the demons and their motives.
- Write your own poem, using the first five lines of this poem as a starting point.
- Draw or paint something that represents the demons lurking behind a smiling face.

— Other Worlds

When you live in a world,
That you don't understand,
It's hard not to reach out,
With a shaking tired hand,
To a world that makes sense,
Though you know that it's wrong,
Because this is a world,
Where you sing the song.

This is a world
Where life makes sense to you,
Where the things people say,
And the things people do,
Don't feel distant and foreign;
Instead they feel right,
You wear this world like a glove,
And you snuggle it tight.

But you know that it's wrong,
And you know it won't pay,
To live in this world,
For the rest of your days.
But for now it feels safe,
So you'll stay for today.
Maybe tomorrow,
You'll find a new way.

Exploring this poem in a therapeutic setting

Questions

- How did you interpret this poem – what world do you imagine the poet refers to?
- What other worlds might the poet be referring to?
- Why do these worlds feel safe?
- What is the alternative to embracing these worlds?
- Why does the poet think it's wrong to live in these worlds?

Extension activities

- Use poetry or prose to describe the world the poet alludes to.

- Do you have a world like this in your life? Describe what is tempting about living there and also explore reasons why you think you shouldn't.

- Imagine the conversation that a good friend might have with someone who is tempted to live in one of the worlds the poet describes. What would a supportive friend say or do?

The Same but Different

We're the same,
But different,
You and I.
You cannot laugh.
I cannot cry.

To you, the world is humourless,
Dark and full of woe.
To me, the world is dangerous,
No place for tears to flow.
You cannot get to sleep at night;
I can't get up when it's dawn.
Your anxious thoughts keep you awake;
My numbness makes me yawn.

We're the same,
But different,
You and I.
You cannot laugh.
I cannot cry.

Exploring this poem in a therapeutic setting

Questions

- In what ways are they the same?

- In what ways are they different?

- Do you think other people would perceive the two subjects of the poem similarly or differently? Why?

- Can you identify with any of the feelings or behaviours described in the poem?

- What causes people to think and respond in this way? Is there always a cause?

Extension activities

- Think of some more ways in which the people portrayed in the poem might be the same and different.

- Work through a fairly typical day of yours and think about how differently someone who is depressed might respond to someone who is anxious at various trigger points. Would the trigger points be the same for each person?

- Write two more verses for the middle of this poem.

— *Always Falling*

Falling,
Always falling.
And never getting up.
Each time she fell further.
The impact doubled with each blow.
The ground no longer solid and reliable,
Her feet her sworn enemies
And no more her trusted guides.
At first, she fought the falls.
But not for long.
No. Not for long.

Exploring this poem in a therapeutic setting

Questions

- What is this poem about?

- How did it make you feel?

- Does the form of the poem on the page impact on your interpretation of it?

- 'At first, she fought the falls. | But not for long.' Why?

- Why does the impact double with each blow?

Extension activities

- Rewrite this poem into one that rhymes.

- Describe in poetry, prose or with drawing how falling feels.

- What advice do you think that someone who cared for the subject would give her? How could she find a way to stop falling? Should she?

Eating disorders and body image

—— Please Eat

The thing is
That I can't.
You think I should.
You think I can.
But I can't.
I don't know if I want to…
You use logic to persuade me
Alluding to futures that I can't imagine,
That I'm scared of,
That could be full of failure.
You tell me that I can
Because I'm strong.
But I don't, because
I'm stronger than you think.
I will…
One day.
But for now, I simply can't.

Exploring this poem in a therapeutic setting
Questions

- Is there anything in this poem that makes a lot of sense to you, or that you do not understand at all?

- Why is the answer to 'Please eat', 'I can't'?

- This poem is very black and white – can vs can't, do vs don't – why do you suppose this is?

- Is it really this black and white or are there shades of grey that haven't been considered here?

- How do you imagine the subject of the poem felt as they made these statements?

Extension activities

- Think about the steps that would need to be taken to move the subject from 'I can't' to 'I can' – who could support with this?

- Play around removing or altering words and grammar in this poem to give it a completely different meaning – can you change it into a positive poem about recovery?

- Write a poem or a list of all the things that you currently feel you can't do. Take one of those things and brainstorm out ways in which you could be supported to change it into a can do. Who or what could support you? What are the potential hurdles and challenges? Tackle more than one if you feel able to.

A Father's View

He watched her sleeping.
A baby again,
With not a care in the world.
But the moment she woke,
Her world would cave in on her.
Make it almost impossible for them both to breathe.

Never had he felt so helpless.
He tried to help.
He tried.
So hard.
He'd coax and cajole.
Just a mouthful…
He'd try to understand,
See things through her eyes;
But before too long,
Care would make way for desperation,
And they'd be screaming.
Again.

Him,
Because he couldn't bear to watch his baby die.
To watch her starve herself to death,
And ravage her body with laxatives.
Her,
Because she couldn't bear to lose control.
To submit to the weight gain
Needed if she wanted to live.

Both of them desperate.
Neither wanting to hurt the other,
Both succeeding
In inflicting deep pain.
Both had aged,
Ravaged by her disease.

He must not let it win.
He must not.
This much he knew.
Of the rest,
He was less sure.

Exploring this poem in a therapeutic setting

Questions

- How does reading this poem make you feel?

- What are the challenges faced by the parent of someone with an eating disorder?

- 'Both had aged, | Ravaged by her disease.' Explore what this means with reference to the daughter and then to the father. What is the same, what is different?

- How do you think the daughter would respond to her father's notion that 'he couldn't bear to watch his baby die'?

- How do you think the father would respond to his daughter's notion that 'she couldn't bear to lose control'?

Extension activities

- The poem starts gently and hopefully and ends distressed and unsure – imagine how this rollercoaster of emotions might play out between parent and child on a daily or weekly basis. What would be the highlights and the lowlights of a typical week?

- The poem says that neither father nor daughter wish to hurt each other, but both are succeeding on inflicting deep pain on the other. Write a list of ways in which they are hurting one another then brainstorm some ways that they could ease this hurt – try to be realistic.

- Consider ways in which this relationship is positive, and ways in which it is negative – consider it from both the point of view of the parent, and the child. Consider ways in which this relationship could be supported or strengthened.

— Conversation with an Anorexic

I'm so fat and I hate it,
I just want to die,
She said as she carefully
Avoided my eyes.
Everyone stares,
Just because I'm so fat,
Nobody cares,
I have an illness that,
People think is my fault,
That's it's all in my head,
But I can't change my thoughts,
And soon I'll end up dead,
Because eating's like poison,
I choke on each bite,
I simply can't do it,
I know it's not right,
But the voice in my head,
Keeps on urging me on,
And I get such a buzz,
Each time more weight is gone.
I love the control,
And I love that I'm good,
At this illness that's eating me,
I thought that it would
Just be a few weeks,
Whilst I lost a few pounds,
But I found it addictive,
And I know that that sounds
Crazy, ridiculous…

No it doesn't.
I say,

But only because I was once,
Just the same way.
I know that to others her words
Seem bizarre;
But to me they're just words that
Describe how things are.
To me they are words that
Describe how things were,
When I was afraid of my food,
Just like her.
And I know that she's honest,
And just saying what she sees,
When she says that she's fat,

Despite the fact that her knees
Are like knots in some string,
And her legs are like birds',
I could tell her,
But there would be no point in my words.
When you're trapped in that world,
There's no easy way home,
And you think they're all lying,
And you feel so alone,
They tell you you're thin,
So they can make you fat,
But the last thing you'd EVER
Want to do would be that.
It must be so hard…
Are the words that I say,
But they're not the right ones,
And in no way portray,
The depth of emotion,
That I feel as she speaks
As I sit here observing her,
Broken and weak.
Yes it is.
She admits,
But she can't make it better,
She just isn't ready
And whilst others can't let her
Continually starve herself,
And neglect her own needs,
I've been there and know she
Will only succeed,
When she's ready
To find her way out of this mess
Which is eating her mind,
And her life,
And her flesh.

Exploring this poem in a therapeutic setting

Questions

- Do you think that only people who had suffered like the girl in the poem had could understand how she feels and the way she behaves? Why/why not?

- The girl is anorexic. What do you think of this line: 'Everyone stares, | Just because I'm so fat.'

- Do you think everyone does stare? Why?

- The poem has a very 'us and them' feel about it – do you think this dichotomy is a true reflection of how things are?

- Do you think it's true that the girl in the poem can only get better when she's ready? Why/why not?

Extension activities

- What makes the girl feel the world is against her? What might help her to view things differently – is it important or helpful that she does?

- If the girl can only get better when she's ready, think about the different challenges that she may face before she feels ready. How might these be overcome? Who or what could support?

- Write a similar poem that is a conversation between yourself and someone who really understands. Pick out and discuss the salient themes that emerge from your poem and use it as an opportunity for self-reflection.

Boy Anorexic

For weeks or months,
They didn't know,
Just quite what could be wrong.
If he'd been a girl, of course,
It wouldn't take so long.
To come to a conclusion
About why he seemed to shrink,
But as a boy, this illness
Was the last thing that they'd think
To test for – no one asked him,
Why he seemed to fade away,
They just took bloods and poked him,
Could be viral? They would say.
And all the time he starved himself,
And dark thoughts ruled his mind.
This half-life he was living
Made him feel deaf and blind
To the world that lived around him,
Folks that didn't know his name.
His name was anorexia,
Or at least that was his game.
A daily game that tortured him
And played him like a toy,
They didn't help,
They didn't know
It could happen to a boy.

Exploring this poem in a therapeutic setting

Questions

- Why would no one suspect that the boy in the poem may be suffering with anorexia?

- Do you think there are differences between male and female people suffering with anorexia – what thoughts and behaviours do you think would be different and what would be the same?

- Do you suppose the boy knew what the problem was? How do you suppose he felt?

- How do you think everyone felt when they eventually worked it out?

- The poem talks about anorexia as a game – who is the player and who is being played? How might different people interpret these roles?

Extension activities

- Write a poem or piece of prose from a parent, doctor or other person in the boy's life which explores how they feel when he is finally diagnosed.

- Write a diary entry exploring how the boy would feel when he finally received a diagnosis of anorexia.

- Expand on the idea of anorexia playing a game in a poem of your own.

— Recovery

She'd fought and won.
That's what they said,
But what they couldn't know,
Was that each and every meal time,
Dealt another blow,
To a thin veneer she'd painted on,
In the hope that she could pass,
For someone who was coping,
With no more need to fast.

You couldn't tell by looking,
That she had a problem now,
She'd gained some weight,
And forced a smile
And made them all so proud.
They thought she'd got it beaten,
And so how could she say,
That despite the fact her clothes fit now
Her hurt was here to stay?

Exploring this poem in a therapeutic setting

Questions

- How does this poem make you feel?

- Do you think people really think that when our bodies look better our minds must be healed too? Why?

- Why does she force a smile?

- The poem says the girl has made everyone proud by gaining weight. How do you imagine she feels about this?

- The girl has chosen not to say anything about how she really feels; do you think this is the right choice?

Extension activities

- If the girl in the poem chose to be honest with someone about how she is feeling now who would be a good person to talk to? Think of as many different possibilities as you can then consider the pros and cons of each.

- How might this conversation go? Imagine, write or role play it. Consider the potential challenges and how these might be overcome.

- Write a poem, a piece of prose or a diary entry which explores how the girl really feels at the moment.

— FAT

They looked at her
And they saw a fat girl.
The kids taunted.
The adults sighed.
She should eat less,
The kids whispered.
She should exercise more,
Said adults in muted tones.
She heard every word.
Lazy.
Greedy.
F A T.
The words of others taunted her daily.
So she comforted herself.
With food.
She knew she shouldn't.
But she couldn't
Stop.

Each mouthful
Faster than the last,
Trying to numb the pain.
Pain she couldn't explain.
Couldn't talk about.
Couldn't even begin to think about.
Guilt with every mouthful.
But no control.
Finally,
Some relief,
Some numbing of pain,
Amidst her feeding frenzy.
Then,
Bloated,
Disgusted,
Fat,
She would stop.
And cry tears of despair.

She should eat less,
The kids whispered.
She should exercise more,
Said adults in muted tones.
She heard every word.
But she couldn't stop.

Exploring this poem in a therapeutic setting

Questions

- Why can't the girl eat less and exercise more like everyone says she should?

- How does food make the girl feel?

- How do you imagine the girl's reliance on food as a means of emotional management started?

- 'Trying to numb the pain. | Pain she couldn't explain. | Couldn't talk about. | Couldn't even begin to think about.' – how did these lines of the poem make you feel?

- It sounds like people talk more about the girl than to her – is this something you can identify with? How do you think it would make her feel?

Extension activities

- Write a list of different strategies the girl might use to manage her emotions other than food.

- It seems the girl is in a vicious cycle where a key trigger for her eating is people calling her fat. Consider what would need to change in order for this cycle to be broken. What first steps might a supportive friend or therapist suggest?

- Rewrite this poem so that it rhymes.

— *Anorexia*

It'll kill you.
They told me.
I couldn't care less.
The thing that I knew,
But I could not confess,
Was that unless it killed me,
Then I'd always know,
That there'd been,
Just a little bit,
Further
To go.

Exploring this poem in a therapeutic setting

Questions

- What were your first thoughts on reading this poem?
- Does the way the poem is laid out on the page impact on the way you interpret it as a reader?
- Why is it that the subject 'couldn't care less' if anorexia killed them?
- Do you think the subject of the poem is suicidal?
- Do you think the subject wants their anorexia to kill them?

Extension activities

- Think about control – who is in control here, the subject of the poem or their anorexia? What might change the balance of power?
- Write a poem in response to this poem from the point of view of someone who disagrees.
- Write your own poem using the first two lines of this poem as a starting point.

Grandmaster or Life?

Anorexia is a game I play
Each day;
A game which requires a lot of pieces.
It is chess.
Always
I am thinking several moves ahead.
I am not a grandmaster yet,
But I know that I could be.
The promise is there.
I have played for many years,
Though I have rarely dedicated myself as I should.
A grandmaster dedicates themselves
Every day.
Chess is their first thought.
Every day.
How to move those pieces…
But I relinquish my pieces;
Willingly I share them
With my husband,
My friend,
And my therapist.
I hand the pieces over.
Help me play the game,
I say,
Passing them rooks and knights,
Removing them from my own hands,
Knowing as I do so that I can manipulate my allies
Into helping me to play the game,
Or,
I can let them teach me a new game.
A new game would be good
I say.
But I'm not sure.
They want me to learn a new game.
Need me to;
Chess is an old game.
It's tiring to watch,
And they do not want to see me end
At checkmate.
Undecided,
I try to learn their game.
Their rules.
It is a less beautiful game
By far.

It is less complicated,
And it never seems to end.
It is not satisfying to play,
Though perhaps that is because
I am an amateur?
I will try,
But I will keep a spare set of chess pieces.
I can choose to play chess if I wish to
And each day,
I will take out those pieces,
And polish them,
And decide whether to place them on the board.
Grandmaster?
Or life?
I will decide,
Each and every day.

Exploring this poem in a therapeutic setting

Questions

- What are your thoughts on the poem's first line: 'Anorexia is a game I play'?
- How do you think the subject feels about the idea of learning a 'new game'?
- Why does the subject choose to keep a spare set of pieces? Is it a good idea?
- The poem implies that recovery is a task to be revisited daily rather than something to be done once. Do you agree?
- The use of the term 'Grandmaster' implies a sense of pride in being a 'good anorexic' – discuss your thoughts on this.

Extension activities

- Write a list of pros and cons for learning a new game vs mastering the old one.
- List all the people that could support when we are learning a new game and what role they might play.
- Imagine a time in the future where the subject has learnt the new game. Write a letter from their future self to their current self which explains why learning a new game is preferable to continuing to play the current game.

—— *Hollows*

Hollows where hollows should not be
Collect rainwater,
Shower water,
Tears.
Everyone looks at those hollows
In horror,
But they bring me solace.
That little pool of water,
Of tears,
Helps to calm
The voices
Who coax the growing
Of those hollows.
I fear my hollows
Will recede.
They must,
Or I will be lost.
But
They calm me so.

Exploring this poem in a therapeutic setting

Questions

- What images come to mind as your read this poem?

- What do you think other people think of the subject's 'hollows'?

- Why does the subject find their hollows calming?

- Who are the voices 'Who coax the growing | Of those hollows.'?

- The subject acknowledges that the hollows should not be there, and yet they like them – do you imagine they feel any conflict over this?

Extension activities

- Think about a typical day and imagine how the subject of this poem might feel at different times.

- Consider a range of different ways that the subject could feel calm as opposed to as a result of observing their hollows.

- Think about how the subject would feel if they gained weight and their hollows became less pronounced. How could these feelings be managed?

The Girl and the Mirror

I see you check the mirror,
And you don't like what you see.
It's clear you think you're ugly.
You don't see things clearly.

You touch a finger to your face,
Smooth creases that aren't there.
Put concealer on imagined spots,
A hand runs through your hair;
It's perfect but you comb it hard,
Smoothing bumps that aren't.
You try to move away then,
From your face but find you can't.

Your attention's been distracted,
By your hatred of your nose,
You poke it, tears in your eyes,
Your anguish clearly shows;
Painted right across your face,
Which just moments before,
I'd found myself admiring,
I can't admire it any more.
Your face, no less than perfect,
How I'd love to look that way,
But the hatred that you feel for it
Makes your beauty go away.

Before my eyes, as I watched on
You looked upon your face,
And destroyed your perfect beauty,
Leaving hatred in its place.

Exploring this poem in a therapeutic setting

Questions

- Why does the girl think she's ugly?
- Is this girl unusual in feeling this way about her reflection?
- What impact do you imagine the application of makeup has on how the girl feels?
- Why do you think the observer is so moved by watching the girl's sadness about her appearance?

- What does the observer mean by 'Your face no less than perfect, | How I'd love to look that way, | But the hatred that you feel for it | Makes your beauty go away'.

Extension activities

- Think about the clothes or make up that you wear and how these reflect on how you feel about yourself – do you think that other people would observe these things in the same way?

- If you usually wear makeup, imagine (or actually try) going for a day without wearing it. How do you think this would make you feel? Do you think it would change the way other people feel about or respond to you?

- Write a poem or piece of prose told from the point of view of the girl on the bus.

— Scales

When I stand on the scales,
The numbers I see,
Feel like a total
Reflection of me.
If they've gone down,
I am strong, brave, successful.
If they've gone up,
I'm a failure, ugly, miserable.

Each day I'm judged
By this inanimate thing,
That shows only numbers
With a razor-sharp sting.
Those numbers can mutate
A good day into bad,
And in the space of one moment
Steal the good thoughts I had.

But what about days
When I've cheated the scales,
And the numbers are down?
The achievement soon pales…
As I set a new goal,
And raise the bar high,
And think myself fat;
My smile fades and I cry.

When you're locked in a battle
With the scales
You can't win.
You lose every day,
And in turn you begin
To lose little bits of yourself,
As the weight
Falls away,
With your life,
Stealing love,
Leaving hate.

Exploring this poem in a therapeutic setting

Questions

- Do you agree with this poem's portrayal of scales?
- Why does the poem state that you can't win?

- Do most people respond to scales in the way the poem describes?

- What would happen if we remove the scales – how might this impact on someone's thoughts, feelings and behaviours?

- How would it impact on someone's daily life to no longer feel this way about the number on the scales?

Extension activities

- If you are in the habit of regularly weighing yourself, keep a note of what you think and feel before and after weighing – compare and contrast this to what is expressed in the poem.

- Write your own poem or piece of prose that reflects how you would like to feel when using scales.

- Choose the four lines of this poem that most resonate with you and incorporate them into a poem of your own.

— If You Could See What I See

Some days,
I wish
I could take a mirror
To your face,
That lets you see
What I see.

Mirrors scare you.
Fear,
Hatred,
And despair
Stare back
Into your haunted,
Desperate eyes.

It's lies.
Your mirror is broken.
It's not you
You see
But an imposter.
Ugly.
Inside and out.

With my mirror,
My eyes,
Finally, you could see yourself
As you really are.
You'd blush,
Bashful,
Your eyes assaulted with beauty
Inside and out.

Exploring this poem in a therapeutic setting

Questions

- Do you know anyone who you could apply this poem to – a friend who doesn't see themselves in the way that you do?
- Can you imagine sharing this poem with a friend – how do you suppose they'd respond?
- Do you think any of your friends would say this could be applied to you?
- Why do we see ourselves differently to how other people perceive us?
- The poem mentions beauty inside, and out – which is more important and why? Which is more valued by society and why?

Extension activities

- Share this poem with a friend or family member.
- Write two descriptions of a friend, one as you think they see themselves, and one as you see them.
- Write a description of yourself as you hope your friends see you – do you believe you're that person? Why/why not?

Shopping for Magic

Carefully,
She picked her way through the rails.
Each garment another disaster.
Another way to feel ugly.
But yet she searched,
In the vain hope
There was magic here.
A way to feel good.
She knew she would fail.
And yet,
She tried.

Exploring this poem in a therapeutic setting

Questions

- What is the poem about?

- How does what we wear impact on how we think and feel?

- The subject seems sure that everything will make her feel ugly and yet she perseveres – why?

- Is it important to keep trying even in the face of failure? Are there times when we shouldn't?

- Where else might the girl find magic if not in the clothes shop?

Extension activities

- Imagine the girl finds the 'perfect' outfit – what would it look like and how would she feel as she put it on and looked in the mirror?

- Use this poem as the basis of a poem that rhymes.

- Take your favourite line or two from this poem and use them as the basis for writing a poem of your own.

Obsessions, compulsions and intrusive thoughts

— Intrusive Thoughts

The ebb and flow of thoughts became too much.
His mind was never empty for a day,
He wondered would this always be the way?
Would he forever fear the things he touched?
He didn't know but hoped that things could change,
He tried so hard to calm the inner words,
But he could not forget them once he'd heard…
The things that they demanded were deranged.
And yet he found that he would be compelled
To follow through on what the voices said
A part of him knew they were in his head
A part of him was transfixed by their spell
It didn't make him happy but he knew,
For now he must do what they told him to.

Exploring this poem in a therapeutic setting

Questions

- What were your first thoughts on reading this poem?
- What form might the subject's intrusive thoughts take?
- What impact might these thoughts have on his day-to-day life?
- Why does he feel compelled to obey the voices in his head?
- Why can he not forget the words once he's heard them?

Extension activities

- List different ways he could try to 'calm the inner words'.

- Explore the real-life consequences of either obeying or failing to obey the inner voices.

- Write a piece of prose or poetry exploring how the subject of the poem would like his life to be – what might recovery look like?

The Voice of Hate

Each day was punctuated
By the voice of hate.
Self-hate.
A voice so loud,
She could hear little else.
Ever critical,
Unresting,
Demanding
And scornful
The voice was not quiet
For even a moment.

She tried to please the voice,
But the voice was never pleased.
Goalposts moved,
Old goals mocked,
And she found herself again,
And again,
And again,
Locked in a cycle of self-hate.
The only party to a voice
No one else would understand.
And she hated it,
As much as it hated her.
And yet,
She listened…

Exploring this poem in a therapeutic setting
Questions

- Why does she listen even though she hates the voice?

- Why is she 'locked in a cycle of self-hate'?

- Do you think it's true that 'no one else would understand'? Why?

- What do you imagine the reactions of friends, family or medical professionals might be if she told them what she was experiencing?

- The unrelentless nature of the voice sounds tiring – do you think it would be?

Extension activities

- Write a dialogue between the girl and the voice – what would she want to say to it?
- Explore the range of emotions the girl may experience in relation to the voice. Consider what makes each of these emotions helpful or unhelpful.
- Write a poem or a piece of prose from the point of view of the voice. Find an inventive way to destroy it.

— Recovering Fate

Do you ever get the feeling
That your thoughts are not your own,
That the things you see, were seen before,
And now you're being shown?

Do you ever get the feeling
That you really don't decide,
Where your feet are taking you,
You just sit back, enjoy the ride?

Do you ever get the feeling
That no matter what you try,
Someone's made their mind up,
If today you'll laugh or cry?

I don't ever get that feeling
Because deep inside I know,
That today can be a good day;
If I fight to make it so.

Exploring this poem in a therapeutic setting

Questions

- Do you think that your actions are predetermined or can we really exert control over how each day goes?

- What can make it feel like your thoughts, feelings and actions are predetermined?

- How can you feel more in control?

- How can we fight to make today a good day?

- Is there a problem with sitting back and enjoying the ride sometimes?

Extension activities

- Consider different ways in which you might get your days off to a positive start. Try implementing them for a few days.

- Keep a diary for a week and consider carefully each day which parts of the day you felt more or less in control of and how comfortable you feel about that.

- Write a poem in response to this poem which argues a different point of view. Discuss the two poems side by side.

Imaginary Friends

You've got these friends,
That we can't see,
Is that normal
When you're three?
I only ask,
Because, you see,
If you weren't three,
I'm sure that we
Would worry
For your mental health,
And take you off
With measured stealth,
To shrinks,
And folk who nod and smile,
Jotting notes and making files,
Deciding what to label you,
Whilst we would worry
…What to do?
But you are three,
And so I think,
That we can live
Without a shrink,
Without a label and concern,
But at what age
Do these friends turn
From playmates into
Mental woes,
When is it that,
Friends become foes?
I ask because I'm puzzled, see,
Why is it okay when you're three,
But never okay later on,
Why prescribe drugs 'til friends are gone?

Exploring this poem in a therapeutic setting

Questions

- Is it okay for a child to have imaginary friends?

- At what age does it become an issue?

- Is it okay to have imaginary friends as an adult if they are kind? What about talking to yourself?

- Many people have internal (or spoken) dialogues with themselves. At what point should this be a cause for concern?

- What do people who have never experienced them think about visual and auditory hallucinations?

Extension activities

- Write a short dialogue between the child in the poem and their imaginary friend. Translate this dialogue so it could be the conversation of adults. Consider how these two different scenarios might be interpreted by others – where the adult interaction is unharmful, would other people be worried?

- Consider other thoughts, feelings and behaviours which are considered acceptable or appropriate for young children but which when experienced in adults cause concern and explore why this is.

- Write a poem or a piece of prose which explores the world of an adult living in a world full of pretend friends, perhaps where the line between imagination and reality is very blurred.

Invasive Thoughts

What if the thoughts you had were not your own,
But thoughts of other people in disguise,
Their thoughts where yours should be, and your thoughts blown
To someplace else, behind some other's eyes.

How could you tell? What would betray those thoughts?
And let you know they weren't your own at all?
That they had trespassed where they were not sought,
Would you feel incomplete and frail and small?

Or maybe you would welcome thoughts of those,
More accomplished and diverse in thought than you,
You could even adapt them if you chose,
And make those thoughts your own, their owner you.

And yet I think no matter how divine,
The only thoughts in my head should be mine.

Exploring this poem in a therapeutic setting

Questions

- What did this poem make you think and feel?

- The structure and rhyming scheme of the poem is very rigid. Do you think this helped or hindered the message it was attempting to convey?

- Have you ever experienced the feeling that your thoughts were not your own?

- How differently might we respond to thoughts that we feel are intruding compared to those we truly own and feel?

- How could we tell the difference between our own thoughts and those of another?

Extension activities

- Write a short story about mind control and explore how intrusive thoughts might be planted and what the consequences might be. Really use your imagination, then stop and consider how it would feel to really believe this kind of version of the truth.

- Rewrite this poem, or a version of it, to give the rhythm and rhyme a more relaxed feel.

- Keep a diary of your thoughts for a few days. Explore the evidence that they are your own. Consider how it feels to own your thoughts – both the good and the bad.

Self-harm

Fading Scars

There was a time
When I hated the scars,
Criss-crossing,
Ragged,
Raw.
Telling my story
To those who cared to see.
Ashamed,
I covered them,
Hid them from view
Hid them from the judgement of the World.
Time has passed,
Things have changed,
My scars have faded.
The scars I grew to hate.
But now I miss them.
A part of my past
Is slowly fading,
Just as I'm ready
To own it.

Exploring this poem in a therapeutic setting
Questions

- Why do you think the poet's attitudes towards their scars have changed?
- Why do you suppose the poet used to hate their scars?
- How can scars tell a story?
- Was the poet right to hide their scars?

- Why was the poet scared of judgement? What do people think when they see this type of scar?
- Do you think the poet's pain faded with their scars?
- Should we hide our scars?
- What advice would you give to this poet?
- Is it good or bad that the poet feels ready to own their past?

Extension activities

- Extend this poem by writing a preceding verse which talks about how the poet felt about their injuries before they healed.
- Set up a debate about whether self-harm injuries or scars should be covered or not.
- Consider the difference between scars resulting from accidental injury and scars resulting from self-harm. Are either or both a significant contributor to our sense of self?
- Write a poem about your feelings about your own scars.
- Tell the story of one of your scars.

— *Again...*

His arms were a mess,
But he couldn't care less
As he got out his old blade again.

He had no other way
To manage hard days,
So his arms paid the price yet again.

He hated the way that his body was wrecked,
But he hated himself and had no self-respect,
So he turned to his razor again.

One day things must change,
But he knew he'd feel strange,
But perhaps he'd be happy again?

Exploring this poem in a therapeutic setting

Questions

- Do you like this poem? Why/why not?

- Why do you think the poet makes repeated use of the word 'again'?

- Why does the subject keep returning to self-harm?

- The subject always uses the same blade to self-harm – why would he do this? What are the dangers with this?

- The subject can see a future where he stops self-harming and is happy – what is stopping him from making that happen?

Extension activities

- The subject repeatedly turns to self-harm to manage difficult moments. What needs to change to break this cycle?

- The subject of the poem has no self-respect so has no hesitance about self-harming. Consider how a past or future version of himself might feel about his self-harm. What might a friend say?

- The subject has no other way to manage his feelings – write a list of as many different ways as you can think of that might help. Would any of these work for you?

Conversation with a Self-Harmer

'My blood is my tears.'
I heard her say,
But it made no sense;
Is there no other way
Of expressing the hurt
And the pain within,
Than taking a blade
To your porcelain skin?

'It makes me feel real.'
She went on to explain,
She felt numb and unreal,
Until she felt pain.
And the pain reassured her,
That she was alive,
And some days it was
All she could do to survive.

'I don't want to die
But I just cannot cope.'
She explained that the cutting
Was a symbol of hope;
That whilst she was cutting,
She was still alive,
That without cutting to cope,
Her resolve would soon dive,
That she might not be able,
To see the day through.
That made sense to me,
Does it make sense to you?

Exploring this poem in a therapeutic setting

Questions

- Does it make sense to you?
- Opinion changes as the conversation goes on – is this positive or negative?
- Why do people struggle to understand why someone would self-harm?
- Do you think the person in the poem wants to stop self-harming?
- Why does she see cutting as a 'symbol of hope'?

Extension activities

- The person in the poem sees her cutting as a 'symbol of hope'. How might other people see it? Consider the viewpoint of several different people, for example a friend, a partner, a child, a parent, a teacher, a doctor, a passer-by, another person who self-harms.

- Make a list of the positives and negatives of self-harm for the person in the poem. How many of these can you relate to? What might you add for yourself?

- Write a companion poem which illustrates the other side of this conversation.

Finding Ways to Belong

Fading scars told the world
He was willing and strong,
That in recovery
He'd found ways to belong.

He'd fought hard and survived.
Well he'd tried,
How he'd tried.
But the scars that were fading
Told lie after lie.
He was no longer cutting,
But still no more alive.

Each day was a struggle,
Each heartbeat a chore,
He had hoped when he stopped
That he'd feel something more
Than a nagging resentment
Of good times gone bad,
And a fear he was destined
To always feel sad.

Life was harder than ever
Since he turned it around,
But with help,
He kept trying,
Until peace was found.

Exploring this poem in a therapeutic setting

Questions

- Why do fading scars make the world think the subject of the poem is strong?
- Why does he not feel strong?
- Why is life 'harder than ever'?
- What do you think he wants to do next?
- Is it worth persevering? Why/why not?

Extension activities

- Write a letter from the boy in the poem to the people in his life who think he's strong. Use it to explain to them how he really feels and perhaps explore what they can do and say to help him feel supported.

- Consider how those who have been concerned about the subject of the poem are feeling now he is apparently in recovery – write a few sentences or words to summarise their feelings then consider how this response might change if they read this poem or his letter. What could they do next?

- Write a poem or a piece of prose about the reality of recovery.

Fresh Blood

He knew no way to manage
That wasn't this way,
And always,
If he found that he'd had a bad day,
He reached out for his blade
And then out his pain played
In the wounds he created
And the hurt that he made.
But the hurt that he made
Was a hurt understood,
Unlike pain from within
That hurt more than it should;
But the hurt from outwith
Made the inner hurt ease,
But the outer hurt grew
Spreading like a disease.
Each day was a bad day
Each day brought new scars.
He knew he must stop
Scars don't change
Who you are.

Exploring this poem in a therapeutic setting

Questions

- Is there anything in this poem that you especially identify with or don't understand?

- Why does the subject of the poem find it easier to understand the pain caused by physical than emotional harm?

- What do you think someone who had never self-harmed would think if they read this poem?

- What is meant by 'The outer hurt grew | Spreading like a disease'?

- Discuss the final statement in the poem: 'Scars don't change | Who you are'.

Extension activities

- The poem ends with the words 'Scars don't change | Who you are' – how does this relate to people's perceptions of you – how might the perceptions of different people change depending on whether or not you have scars?

- Create a piece of poetry, prose or art that represents how the boy in the poem is feeling.
- Take four lines of this poem that especially resonate and write your own poem which incorporates them.

Suicide

— By His Own Hand

How could you?
They asked you,
How could you?
But you could not answer
As you were not here.

Why would you?
They asked you,
Why would you?
But their questions fell onto
The world's deafest ears.

I loved you!
They told you,
I loved you.
But they told you too late,
Through their tears.

I'll miss you,
They told you,
I'll miss you.
And in death now
They hold you so dear.

Exploring this poem in a therapeutic setting

Questions

- What has happened?
- Who are 'they'?
- What could have happened to make things turn out differently?

- The poem is a series of questions – do you think this works? Are these questions you can imagine people really thinking or asking?

- What are the different ways that the opening phrase 'How could you?' could be interpreted?

Extension activities

- Write answers to the questions in the poem from the person it is about – what would they want to say and explain?

- Write a list of things that people who care about the subject of the poem could have done to help before it got too late.

- Imagine that the subject of the poem had survived – continue the poem in your own words trying to write some hope into the situation.

That Day

She replayed That Day
Every day.
The little things
She should have said,
Should have done,
To stop it happening.
She knew it was futile;
She could no more go back in time
Than she could levitate.
Besides…
That Day was simply the culmination
Of many days before
Where she had not said,
Had not done,
Had not noticed
What a mother surely should have.
But now That Day had passed,
And all was lost.

Exploring this poem in a therapeutic setting

Questions

- How does this poem make you feel?

- Is there anything here that especially resonates with you?

- Do you think the mother is right for beating herself up and thinking she could or should have done something different?

- 'She replayed That Day | Every Day' – how long do you think this will continue for? Do you think it is helpful or harmful?

- 'That Day was simply the culmination | Of many days before' – what do you think the days or months leading to 'That Day' had felt like for the different people involved?

Extension activities

- What do you think the subject of the poem might want to say to their Mum if they were to learn of the thoughts and feelings in this poem? Write a poem or piece of prose to reflect these thoughts and feelings.

- Write a list of different sources of support that the mother could seek at this time and consider the pros and cons of each and how she might feel about seeking such support.

- Write, draw or paint about 'That Day' and the resulting feelings from the point of view of the subject, the parent or a friend.

—— Beautiful Nature

As she stood,
She admired the beauty
Of the world around her.
The sun, not quite set,
Casting multi-coloured shadows,
Painting pictures on trees and houses.
Birds circling overhead,
Exchanging idle chatter about the day passed.
Trees budding into life with the promise of spring;
She could smell the faint scent of blossom
On the breeze.
As she stood,
Drawing ragged breaths,
Admiring the beauty of the World,
Everything was good,
Just for a moment.
It was almost enough to stop her jumping.
But not quite.

Exploring this poem in a therapeutic setting

Questions

- What did this poem make you think or feel?

- Did you like this poem? Why/why not?

- What is your favourite line of this poem – what do you especially like about that line?

- Which is your least favourite line, why?

- What do you think the poet was trying to achieve when they wrote this poem?

- How can the beauty of nature impact on our mood when we are having especially dark days?

Extension activities

- Rewrite the ending of this poem – what other story could you choose to tell?

- Write a list of the different ways that we can use the power of nature to lift our mood in dark times – are any of these ideas things you could try?

- Create a poem, a piece of prose or a piece of art inspired by some of the images of nature conjured by this poem.

—— Late

Late again!
Bloody train,
It's the third time this week
That my crushing commute
Has had to take a back seat
To signalling issues,
And leaves on the line,
Or not enough drivers.
Trains never on time.
I sit fuming, frustrated,
On platform three.
Why does this always
Happen to me?
Then comes the announcement:
'Sorry for the delay'
But it's not due to leaves
On the line. Not today.
Today a young mother
Has jumped on the tracks.
Today a young mother
Has no going back,
From a decision she took
To say goodbye to life.
It was too hard being Mum
And a young, loving wife.
I reel in my frustration
Kiss my anger goodbye
I'm late
But I'm happy, healthy.
Alive.

Exploring this poem in a therapeutic setting

Questions

- Why does the feel of the poem change so much when we know the nature of the delay?

- What difference would it make if we just knew there had been a 'casualty' rather than having the details of the person who took their life?

- How does it make us feel when we learn of the misfortune of others like this?

- How could the poem better capture these feelings?

- Are there any parts of the poem you particularly like? Why? Any parts you dislike?

Extension activities

- Rewrite the poem imagining that the casualty was a different kind of person – consider the two poems side by side.

- Write separate, short narratives from the point of view of several people touched by the incident, perhaps the casualty, a commuter who is held up on their regular journey, someone who is travelling somewhere urgently, someone who saw it happen and someone who hears about it on the news.

- Sadly, one of the things we will hear exclaimed about someone who ends their life in front of a commuter train is that it is selfish to inconvenience so many others. What do you think about this? Create a poem, a piece of prose or a piece of art that reflects your feelings.

Do Not Fall

Do not fall;
Hold on.
Find a foothold,
A hand,
A voice
Or a memory
That keeps you in the now.
Smell it,
Feel it,
Hear it,
Taste it,
Do not fall;
Hold on.

Exploring this poem in a therapeutic setting

Questions

- What does the poem mean?

- Can you identify with this feeling of needing to hold on?

- What kind of footholds might we be able to use?

- Why does it help to use our senses?

- What if we can't hold on?

Extension activities

- Write a response to this poem, imagining that the subject can hold on and feels more positive.

- Write a response to this poem imagining that the subject cannot hold on and feels hopeless – what could we do to address this?

- Write a list of different ways that you can 'hold on' at a time like this. Consider as many different footholds as possible and think about how you can employ all five senses.

Recovery

The Crest of a Wave

On the crest of a wave,
Would he surf,
Would he fall?
On top of the world,
Or weighed down by it all?
He was up,
He was down,
He was playing the clown,
But behind the façade
Was a deep furrowed frown.
But he aimed to confuse
With his laughs and his jokes
He was surfing a wave,
But his feelings were choked.

Exploring this poem in a therapeutic setting

Questions

- Was there anything about this poem that you could really identify with?
- Do you think that it's normal for recovery to be filled with ups and downs like this?
- How do you suppose the subject of the poem feels on the down days?
- The poem states 'he aimed to confuse' – why?
- Why are his feelings choked?

Extension activities

- This poem uses the analogy of a wave – what other analogies can you think of which reflect your experience of illness and recovery?

- Write a poem or piece of prose based on one of the analogies you have come up with.
- Consider whether this pattern of peaks and troughs is helpful or harmful. Is there anything that the subject of the poem could do to even things out?

Kintsugi (Beauty in Broken)

There is beauty in the broken,
There is hope where there's repair.
Cracks and dark spots bring to life
A work that once was bare.

Craftsman's hands produce a piece
That's perfect, but it's plain
And in our use we break and mark
That piece with love and pain.

And as the years roll by we see
Not cracks, or holes, or marks,
But a piece we've loved and cherished;
With each mark, a memory's sparked.

Exploring this poem in a therapeutic setting

Questions

- What were your first thoughts as you read this poem?

- Do you agree with the notion that there can be beauty in the broken?

- How can we apply this to the process of recovery?

- How can our breaks make us stronger?

- Is perfection ever more beautiful than imperfection?

Extension activities

- Do you think that people change during the process of recovery? How might people change in positive or negative ways?

- Consider the journey that your own recovery is taking you on – what are you proud of and what are the important parts of your journey/lessons learned?

- Write a piece of prose or poetry celebrating someone or something that is broken or who has faced adversity and is now stronger/more beautiful as a result.

Marble in a Jar

She was a marble in a jar,
Pressed amongst
Hard,
Cold marbles,
Struggling to find her way out.
Each time she moved up,
The marbles around her shifted,
Unpredictably,
Until she found herself resting
At the bottom of the jar
Once more.

Exploring this poem in a therapeutic setting

Questions

- How does this poem make you feel?

- What was the poet trying to convey?

- Can you identify with this pattern of feelings?

- What should she do next?

- How would the unpredictable nature of the shifting described in the poem make someone in recovery feel?

Extension activities

- Consider different analogies for recovery – how can you describe your own experience in an abstract way?

- Write a poem or a piece of prose or create a piece of art that portrays your analogy.

- Compare and contrast your analogy with the marble in the jar analogy.

Thinking Forwards

the future eludes me
it looms far and large
i don't understand
how to travel
from where i am now
to a place i've not been
and feel sanity will surely
unravel

Exploring this poem in a therapeutic setting

Questions

- How do you think the poet felt when writing this?
- There is no punctuation in this poem. Do you think this is intentional? Why?
- Why does the future 'loom far and large'?
- Why does travelling somewhere we've not been before make it feel more daunting?
- Will sanity unravel? Why/Why not?

Extension activities

- Rewrite the poem to incorporate punctuation. Compare and contrast the new version of the poem with the old version.
- Write a list of different ways that we can make the future feel less scary – consider which of these you might be able to try yourself.
- The poem expresses concern that sanity will unravel during recovery – how can these fears be allayed? How can this process be supported?

Support and Listening

— Helping Hand

She was hurting
And broken,
Her life in a mess
When a hand
From the darkness
Reached out.

It took her hand gently
And held her a while
And gave her
A reason
To hope.

The hand soon retreated,
But its warmth still remained,
And it gave her
The strength
To try harder.

And so then each day,
She gave way to the strain
Then found strength
In this hand
And got up.

Exploring this poem in a therapeutic setting

Questions

- What did you think of this poem? Was there anything you especially liked or disliked?

- This poem feels like it should rhyme but it doesn't, do you think it should?

- When you first heard the poem, what did you imagine was happening? Has your perception changed at all on rereading?

- What or who do you suppose the hand from the darkness could represent?

- 'The hand soon retreated, | But its warmth still remained,' What is happening here?

- Is it important that we learn to manage our thoughts and feelings independently?

Extension activities

- Think of all the different things or people that might offer a 'helping hand' what are the pros and cons of each – which might you turn to when?

- Rewrite this poem so that it rhymes – how does this change its feel?

- Take your favourite line from this poem and use this as a title for your own poem, piece of prose or piece of art.

Calmer Waters

Ever increasing circles,
The ripples on a pond,
The calming hands of many,
All joined by a bond.
The ocean feels calmer,
The waves start to subside,
Until at last it's far too late
To run away and hide.
But hiding's less important
As the maelstrom desists;
Whilst choppy waters even out,
Friendship's hand persists.

Exploring this poem in a therapeutic setting

Questions

- What is this poem about?

- Is it more helpful to have the helping hands of many or a few? Why?

- How can friends and family support us through difficult times?

- Do you agree that 'hiding's less important | As the maelstrom desists'?

- Does friendship's hand persist?

Extension activities

- Write a list of practical ways that friends and family could offer support during recovery. Consider how you might share these with those who care about you.

- Write a diary entry from the point of view of a friend looking in who doesn't know how best to help. What barriers are there? How might these be addressed?

- Think of a situation in which you felt truly supported – who was supporting you and why did it feel like such a positive experience?

— A Disappointing Visit

They said they cared,
But they were gone.
They left the first moment
That social etiquette dictated they might,
With stilted hugs
And muffled offers of help.

Gone.

In truth,
They were gone before they had arrived.
Their arrival was in body only,
Their spirits had not entered the building;
Warded off by depression,
Dishes not yet washed
And the smell that comes only
Of not caring if you live or die.

She was glad they had gone.
She had awaited the visit with anticipation,
Her disappointment had, if nothing else,
Allowed her to feel a sharp emotion,
Where there had been none.

Exploring this poem in a therapeutic setting

Questions

- How does this poem make you feel?

- Does any of it sound familiar?

- How do you imagine the home of the subject looks, feels and smells based on the poem's description? What impact would this have on visitors?

- What do you think the subject expected from the visit?

- 'Her disappointment had, if nothing else, | Allowed her to feel a sharp emotion, | Where there had been none.' What is the poet trying to express here?

Extension activities

- Write two diary entries from the point of view of one of the visitors – one prior to the visit about their expectations and one after the visit.

- What do you imagine the friends who visited said to each other after the visit? What do you imagine they felt they should do next? Write a dialogue exploring their conversation.

- Consider practical ways that future similar visits could be managed to make them less disappointing.

Self-esteem

Because I could tell
That you meant what you said,
I stayed where I sat and I listened.

Your eyes were sincere,
And your heart on your sleeve,
I could tell that you cared,
So I listened.

I didn't believe
All the things that you said
But I sat down
And carefully listened.

Maybe one day,
I'll believe what you say
But for now I'll just sit here
And listen.

Exploring this poem in a therapeutic setting

Questions

- Who do you think the subject of the poem is listening to?

- Is it important to continue listening? Why?

- Why is the poem called 'Self-esteem'?

- Why does the subject not believe what they are being told?

- Do you think the subject will ever believe good things that are said about them? How might they grow in confidence?

Extension activities

- Consider some specific examples of positive things that people have said about or to you in the past that you have dismissed or disbelieved. Why did you not believe these things and what evidence would you need to believe they were true?

- Write a companion poem from the point of view of the person who is being listened to.

- Explore how it would feel to be able to believe and accept positive things that are said about you.

Listening Ear

You don't listen because you have to,
It's because you really care,
And on more than one occasion
I've been so glad you've been there.
Not much is gained by talking,
Or at least that's how I feel
Before you've sat and listened;
Made the things I say seem real.
It doesn't make it hurt less
But I feel less alone.
When I talk,
And you listen,
I feel I've found my home.

Exploring this poem in a therapeutic setting

Questions

- Does this poem resonate with you at all?

- Why does the subject feel listening won't help?

- Do you think listening does help?

- What makes a good listener?

- Is there anyone who makes you feel listened to? What do they do well?

- 'When I talk, | And you listen, | I feel I've found my home.' What is meant by this?

Extension activities

- Write a list of pros and cons of being listened to. Does this list change depending on who is doing the listening?

- Choose your favourite line of the poem. Talk about why it is your favourite line and how you think the poem would change without it. Do the same with your least favourite line.

- Write your own poem or piece of prose about a time you felt really heard.

— You Didn't Ask

I didn't tell you,
Because you didn't ask.
Perhaps if you had,
I'd have found the words
To ask for help.
But you didn't.

Perhaps if you'd asked,
I'd have told you
About the things he said.
The things he did.
The scars I hid.
But you didn't.

Perhaps if you'd asked,
I'd have cried,
Or pushed you away,
Told you there was nothing
I needed to say.
But maybe not.

I didn't tell you,
Because you didn't ask.

Perhaps you didn't ask,
Because you knew.
And you just didn't
Know what to do.
But nor did I.

You didn't ask.

Exploring this poem in a therapeutic setting

Questions

- How does this poem make you feel?
- Whose point of view do you think the poem is told from and who do you think they are talking to?
- What do you think the poem is about?
- Do you think the use of space and irregular splitting of stanzas is intentional? Is it effective?
- What do you think would have happened if the subject of the poem had been asked?

Extension activities

- Write a dialogue between the two people in the poem which explores what happens when the question is finally asked.

- Create a poem, piece of prose or piece of art that represents the feelings of the person whose viewpoint the poem is told from. Consider in what ways these feelings are helpful or harmful.

— *How Are You?*

Three words so often uttered,
But very rarely meant:
'How are you?'
'How are you?'
'How are you?'
We ask
But the answer
Is breath misspent.

Because nobody cares,
Not really.
Not unless the answer is 'Fine.'
Nobody wants to hear the words
'I'm not okay, do you have some time?'

We don't have time,
Not ever.
Not even for those we love most.
In response to the question:
'How are you?'
We do not expect the verbose.

If the answer is somewhat surprising,
Runs to more than a second or two,
We stand there impatiently waiting
For the respondee to hurry on through.

When we ask after others we don't mean it.
We're really just being polite.
But if you don't want to know,
Please don't ask me.
Or I might tell you I'm not alright.

Exploring this poem in a therapeutic setting

Questions

- What is the point of the poem?

- Do you agree with the poem?

- How do you respond when someone says 'How are you?' – is that how you should respond?

- Can you think of anyone who really means it when they ask how you are? Why do they mean it if others don't?

- Why do people ask 'How are you?' if they aren't interested in the answer?

Extension activities

- Think about people who might recently have asked you 'How are you?' who you told you were 'fine' or similar – how would they feel if they really understood how you were feeling? How would they feel about the fact that you didn't share your true feelings with them?

- Consider whether we too are guilty of asking 'How are you?' without wanting or expecting an answer? How can we change some of our daily interactions so that we say what we mean? Also, when we know a friend is in distress, how can we make it clear that we genuinely care about the answer to our question?

- Use the phrase 'I'm fine' as the basis of a companion poem.

Cuddles: The Best Medicine

Sometimes words don't hit the spot,
But cuddles always do.
They ease our pain,
Relieve our woes
And make us smile too.

It has to be a special hug,
(Not any hug will do)
From one we love,
Who loves us back,
And knows us through and through.

The type of hug can vary,
Depending on what's wrong.
A big bear hug,
A gentle touch,
Or rocking with a song.

We never get too old for hugs,
And don't start off too young.
Those that we love,
And need the most,
Are always tightly clung.

On the days when words won't do,
A cuddle's a good start.
So if you want
To help a friend,
Extend your arms and heart.

Exploring this poem in a therapeutic setting

Questions

- Do you agree?
- Who do you like or dislike being cuddled or held by?
- Why does touch help us when we feel down?
- Are there other kinds of touch that can help us besides a hug?
- How else can we seek this kind of contact when we are not with someone we know or feel comfortable being held by?

Extension activities

- Create a piece of art that shows how it feels to be held.
- Think about the differences between the person who is being held and the person doing the holding. What are the different motivations, thoughts and feelings?
- Take the last line of this poem and use it as the first line of a new poem.

It's Not Easy Being Friends Sometimes

We're here for you,
We know you're blue,
We'll do whatever, we can do.
We understand,
We'll hold your hand,
We know that on your feet, you'll land.
You're still our friend,
Your needs, we'll tend,
Depression won't, our friendship rend.

But it's all lies,
It's no surprise,
When friendship fades and fails and dies.

Exploring this poem in a therapeutic setting

Questions

- Talk about what you think this poem is about and what it refers to.
- Why is it hard to maintain friendships when someone is depressed?
- When friendship fails in this way is it anyone's fault? Is it irretrievable?
- 'It's all lies' – is this true or is there something else going on here?
- Is it possible that people with depression actively push friends away? If so, how and why?

Extension activities

- Consider reasons why friendship might be important when we are suffering with depression. Write as long a list as possible.
- Think about practical things we can do in order to maintain our friendships at difficult times – consider both dos and don'ts. Think of the potential stumbling blocks for each suggestion. Which, if any, of these suggestions would we be able to follow through on even at our lowest points?
- Write a poem or piece of prose from the point of view of a friend who feels they are being pushed away.

—— *Depression*

Think happy thoughts!
She did not understand depression,
But meant well.

Exploring this poem in a therapeutic setting

Questions

- Does this resonate?

- Have you had similar experiences?

- Are there other phrases you have heard which have made you feel misunderstood?

- Why would someone think it helpful to tell someone with depression to 'think happy thoughts'?

- Why did the subject of the poem find it was not helpful?

Extension activities

- Rewrite this poem in a longer form.

- Write a letter from the subject of the poem to the person who told her to 'think happy thoughts' explaining her thoughts and feelings around this phrase (you can choose a live example from your own life if you prefer).

- Write a Haiku which explores your thoughts or feelings today.

Help Me to be a Better Friend

I don't know how to be with you,
I don't know what to say.
I want to be a help to you,
But you push everyone away.

I know that things are hard right now,
And that you feel alone,
You cannot bear my company,
But feel sad on your own.

Please tell me what to say or do,
To be a better friend,
I'm happy to take orders,
To help your head and heart to mend.

Can I wash the dishes?
Take the dog out for a walk?
Maybe when you're ready,
I can listen whilst you talk?

Just tell me what to do please,
As I worry every day,
That my efforts are pathetic
As you slowly ebb away.

I care about you deeply,
And I really want to try,
To be a better friend to you,
And help you through this time.

Exploring this poem in a therapeutic setting

Questions

- Do you think the person from whose viewpoint the poem is told is a good friend, or a bad friend? Why?

- Could they be a better friend? How?

- How do you think they are feeling right now?

- Would you like a friend like this? Do you have one?

- The rhyme and rhythm of this poem make it feel a lot less serious than the content would normally dictate. Do you think this is a good or a bad thing?

Extension activities

- Write a list of practical ways that the friend could help out.
- Explore ways in which the person writing the poem could support the friend they are worried about.
- Rewrite this poem so it no longer rhymes and has a less regular rhythm.

Trying to Help

Why won't you talk to me?
I know there's something wrong,
I want to help, I really do
But I fear I've not got long.

You're slipping far away from me,
More distant with each day,
I can hear your depth of suffering
As you mutter 'I'm okay'.

You shift your gaze away from me,
Block my touch with your crossed arms,
I wonder what's gone wrong here,
Why you're suffering silent harm.

I think the demons in your head
Refuse to let me help,
I think that they belittle you
And beat you 'til you yelp.

I hope to find a chink soon
In your armour – let me in,
Please say you'll let me listen,
Then the hard work can begin.

Exploring this poem in a therapeutic setting

Questions

- Does this sound familiar?

- Have you ever refused to let people in? Who and why?

- Is it easy to let people in? Why?

- The poem refers to blocking body language – is this something you have observed in yourself or others – is it conscious or unconscious?

- 'Then the hard work can begin' – what does this mean? What comes next?

Extension activities

- Work through the reasons why you, or the person in the poem, might refuse to let people in and consider how each of these could be overcome.

- Consider how the conversation might go if a chink was found.

- Write a poem or piece of prose exploring the feelings of the person to whom this poem is addressed.

— *Kind Words are Not Always Heard*

Sometimes there is no subtext,
We just say what we mean,
But if we say it nicely,
Then the listener's not too keen.
Thinking we don't mean it.
Thinking that we lie.
Thinking that nice words we say
Are insults on the sly.

Some people can't hear compliments;
In positives they hear,
Not good things,
But unpleasant things,
Lurking very near.
It's hard to be persistent.
To keep on being nice,
When the good words you take time to speak,
Are treated like they're lies.
But time and time again we try,
To make our kind words heard,
In the hope that finally, one day,
They'll sink in, every word.

Exploring this poem in a therapeutic setting

Questions

- What did this poem make you think?

- Do you recognise yourself or someone you know in this poem?

- Why do some people find it hard to accept compliments?

- Do you think it's important to be able to accept praise and compliments?

- Are compliments ever a disguise for insults or other unpleasantries?

Extension activities

- Write a list of kind things that people have said to or about you which you have found hard to accept or believe. Consider the evidence that these things may in fact be true.

- Write a poem or a piece of prose which represents the thoughts and feelings of the person who is trying to be kind – how do you think it makes them feel when their kindness is dismissed?

- Imagine what it would be like to be the person that people paint with their kindness and compliments? Would you like to be able to believe you were that person? How could things be different each day if you were?

— Hidden Scars

When did it become so hard,
To tell the truth,
And show our scars?
When did we decide that we,
Must hide our hurt,
Our pain,
And flee,
To distant lands,
Within our heads,
Emotions hidden,
Dulled and dead,
Never to be shared aloud,
Instead we're silent,
Smiling,
Proud.
Proud of juggling life so well,
Proud we manage not to tell,
Proud our lives look good to all,
But pride's what comes before a fall.
And so we hide hurt rather well,
But deep inside it starts to swell,
Until we're taken with the tide,
Of all the things we tried to hide,
And then our secrets are no more,
Our problems spill upon the floor,
Seeping, sliding; making mess,
Whilst others sidestep,
We confess,
We couldn't manage any more.
We hide our scars but they're still raw.

Exploring this poem in a therapeutic setting

Questions

- Do you think this poem is an accurate portrayal?

- Why do we hide our inner hurt?

- What price might we pay when we keep our emotions locked up?

- What is means by the final line 'We hide our scars but they're still raw'?

- What would need to change to make us feel more comfortable being honest about our emotions?

Extension activities

- Take your favourite line from this poem and use it as the starting point for a new poem.
- Create a poem, piece of prose or a piece of art that represents the feelings that result from bottling our emotions up.
- Rewrite this poem so that it doesn't rhyme. How does this change the feel of the poem?

Healing Hold

You melt into my arms,
Your body shaking with sobs,
Your eyes red and raw,
Lost in your tear-streaked,
Snot-stained face.
'Mumma'
You whisper as you nestle your face
Into my shoulder,
Where it fits just right.
You grip me tight with little fingers
And clamp your legs around my waist,
And you breathe deeply,
Slowly,
Calmly,
And the sobs subside.
I do nothing;
I just hold you…
But you heal.
I hope it will always be this way.

Exploring this poem in a therapeutic setting

Questions

- What does this poem make you think and feel?

- How do you think the child feels?

- How do you think 'Mumma' feels?

- Why does the child recover and heal just from being held?

- Where can we find support that feels this good once we are no longer a small child?

Extension activities

- Rewrite this poem so that it rhymes.

- Write a companion poem from the point of view of the child.

- Create a poem, a piece of prose or a piece of art that represents how the child feels during this poem – consider how we can achieve the positive aspects of these feelings for ourselves.

Part Three

Encouraging and enabling therapeutic poetry writing

* * *

As well as exploring the poetry of others, writing our own poetry can be incredibly therapeutic – both if we have first-hand issues we need to work through and also as a form of emotional release if we are supporting others with their problems and find this load is heavy.

Many people find the idea of writing poetry quite intimidating and if you suggest it to someone you're supporting you may be met with some resistance. Below I've outlined some of the commonly perceived barriers to poetry writing and given some ideas to help you enable, encourage and support. I've addressed most of my answers to the poet – this may be you, or it may be someone you're working with, or it may be both.

I've never written a poem before
That's okay – there's a first time for everything and it can often be interesting to learn to do something new. It can often be reassuring for the person you're supporting if you share your own experience. If you've written poetry yourself, talk about how you got started and how you felt at first and how your confidence grew. If you're new to poetry, perhaps now is the time to start, that way you and

your client can learn together which is always infinitely easier than starting on our own.

Reading other people's poems can also really help to build our confidence and help us to hone in on the kind of style we're most comfortable with so we might encourage reading more poetry as a preface to writing our own – perhaps set your client a challenge to bring some poems to one of your discussions that they have found enjoyable or interesting.

I'd rather write prose

That's fine – many of the prompts later in this chapter could be used equally for creating a poem, a piece of prose or a piece of art. Our aim is to use creativity in a supportive way so if you'd feel more comfortable using a different medium then go for it. It is worth revisiting poetry periodically as it may feel like the right thing at some point.

You may prefer to read poetry than to write it – again this is fine – many of the poems included in this book come with suggested extension tasks which do not involve writing your own poems – but if the inspiration ever does take you, then dare to go with it and you may find you begin to enjoy it.

I don't know anything about poetry

It doesn't matter. We're not looking to create masterpieces, we are looking for a way to express and explore feelings. Whilst there are forms (such as Haikus and Sonnets) that you can choose to adhere to if you wish, there are very few rules when it comes to poetry. The rules are up to the individual poet so don't be afraid to set your own rules and then to challenge and break them. The key thing is to feel free to explore your emotions on paper in whatever form feels most comfortable.

You may enjoy learning more about poetry – if so, Stephen Fry's book *The Ode Less Travelled: Unlocking the Poet Within* is an excellent starting point. Alternatively, you could choose to join an online or local poetry group. However, unless you specifically want to learn more about poetry or to communicate with other poets, you may be just as happy spending your time playing with words and form on your own.

What I write will be rubbish

This is completely subjective – but again it doesn't matter. We are not here to discuss the quality of any poetry that is produced, but rather to use it as a way of expressing and exploring emotions, thoughts and feelings. Opinion is often split when it comes to poetry and it's a real case of one man's trash is another man's treasure – this is true of almost any art form. I have written a poem a day, every day for over two years. Many of the finished poems are not works of which I'm hugely proud, but every single one of them either had significance at the time of writing, or sparked conversations following its publication on my blog, or both.

I don't know what to write

This is a common problem and it's a key reason why I've provided a series of prompts in this book to act as starting points. A great habit to get into is to jot down notes any time inspiration strikes. Either carry a notepad or use a note app on a portable device and make yourself a note every single time something strikes you as potential inspiration for a poem. Sometimes it will be an image or words you see which you want to expand on. Sometimes it will be a storyline or conceit for a poem. Sometimes a full verse will arrive fully formed in your mind. Whatever your inspiration, be sure to write it down as even the ideas which you think are completely memorable have a nasty habit of being forgotten very quickly.

Having a few ideas noted means that if you feel the urge to write or find you have the time, then you have some good points to start from.

I don't have time

There is never enough time for everything, but if you want to write poetry then you will find the time. You may find that you grow to enjoy writing or reading poetry and that it is an activity which you wish to prioritise your time for. However, unless you want to, you don't have to find hours of time. Most of my poems are written in under ten minutes. This is largely because I have a routine which sees me writing poetry at the same time each day and I've found I've become faster and faster – this idea could work for you too. Equally, time which isn't always fully utilised like your lunch hour or a regular commute can be a regular chance to put pen to paper. I mostly write my poems on my iPhone perched at the end of my daughter's bed whilst she drifts off to sleep at night. Getting into a habit of writing means that you are exercising your 'writing muscles' so if you give it a go regularly for a little while, you'll find writing becomes easier. If you make a habit of writing at the same time, in the same place each day you may also soon find that your body and mind become accustomed to this routine and start to feel ready to write when you revisit this familiar situation.

I'm too embarrassed to show anyone

You don't have to show your poetry to anyone if you don't want to. Or perhaps you would prefer to share it with a selected one or two people. However, if you do feel you can share your poetry more widely then it can be very interesting to hear other people's interpretations of what you've written – they're often very different to your own and can really get you thinking. You'll often also find that other people find meaning or value in your words and this can be very encouraging. However, if your confidence is very low or the matters of which you write are deeply personal then there is no reason at all why your writing should not be a solely personal endeavour.

Enjoy the process!

Poetry shouldn't be a chore. If it feels that way then stop. You can add to your enjoyment by making your poetry writing feel more special – perhaps by creating a nice relaxing environment with soft music, candles and something good to drink. I am also a sucker for a beautiful notepad and pen though I'll admit that these days just as many of my poems are tapped out on my iPhone on a busy commuter train as are carefully crafted in a more relaxing environment. Find what works for you – remember, you make the rules, but above all, enjoy it.

The following sections include an overview of a few poetic forms which you could try out if you want to, followed by fifty prompts designed to inspire you to get writing. However, feel free to just get writing without reading the following sections if the inspiration and mood take you.

Poetic forms

Before providing specific prompts to inspire poetry writing, I'm going to walk you through a series of poetic forms. This can prove a useful starting point and structure for someone who likes to work with rules or wants to add an additional challenge or bit of structure. You can pick any of these structures for any of your poems. When considering how to extend the work you're doing using the poems in Part Two, or other poems you've sourced, you can always consider rewriting an existing poem in a different form – ask your client, 'Can you try to write a sonnet using the poem we've just read as inspiration?'

For some people working with poetic forms can feel overly formulaic or restrictive and may quell creativity. If you find this to be the case with someone you are working with then feel free never to consider them again. However, some people relish the challenge of creating poems in specific forms. You'll have to feel your way a little and ensure that your client always knows that regardless of any challenges you may have set them to try in their own time, the writing of poetry is something that we hope they would enjoy so if they prefer not to adhere to a specific structure, or they want to adapt it to make it their own, then that is not a problem at all.

The forms I've outlined are not designed to be a comprehensive review of poetic forms but rather a small collection of different types of poem I have personally enjoyed the challenge of writing and which I think you, or your client, may find interesting or fun too. It can be helpful and fun to explore different poetic forms using examples – I have included examples of my own work and many additional examples are available readily online. Sourcing poems written in a specific form and sharing them as part of your discussion can be useful and interesting preparation for a session – or it is something you could do together if you have more time.

Form 1: Haiku

Haiku are short poems that use sensory language to capture a feeling or image. They are often inspired by an element of nature, a moment of beauty or a poignant experience. Haiku poetry was originally developed by Japanese poets, and the form was adapted to English and other languages by poets in other countries.

In English, Haiku tend to have three lines. The first line has five syllables, the second line has seven syllables and the third line has five syllables. It is up to you how strict you choose to be with this form; some people prefer to write Haiku with fewer syllables that can be expressed in one breath.

Haiku Format:

> Line 1: 5 syllables
> Line 2: 7 syllables
> Line 3: 5 syllables

A Haiku usually juxtaposes two ideas separated by a line break, punctuation or space.

Haiku use sensory language – they tend to describe rather than explain. Imagine that the challenge here is to paint a picture with your words.

Tide Turning – Haiku Example

> Sea, lapping, crashing.
> Memories fade, washed away.
> Tide turns… A fresh start.

Nightfall – Haiku Example

> As dark closes in
> The bird calls quieten;
> The night comes alive

An alternative to a Haiku is a Lune (also known as an 'American Haiku') which is based on word rather than syllable count. There are no other rules. It looks like this:

Lune Format:
Line 1: 3 words
Line 2: 5 words
Line 3: 3 words

Depression – Lune Example

Think happy thoughts!
She did not understand depression,
But meant well.

Form 2: Sonnet

A sonnet consists of fourteen lines which are written in iambic pentameter – that means there are ten beats per line: 'dee-dum dee-dum dee-dum dee-dum dee-dum'. They usually rhyme and there are many variations on the specific rhyming schemes that you can choose to use – and you can invent your own, or write a non-rhyming one if you wish.

Two popular rhyming forms are the Shakespearian Sonnet and the Petrarchan Sonnet.

Shakespearian Sonnet Format:

A B A B | C D C D | E F E F | G G

I often choose to play with this and write my sonnets in the format:

A B B A | C D D C | E F F E | G G

Petrarchan Sonnet Formats:

A B B A | A B B A | C D C D | C D
A B B A | A B B A | C D E C | D E
A B B A | A B B A | C C D C | C D
A B B A | A B B A | C D D C | E E

Don't be afraid to play around to find the rhyme scheme and pattern of line breaks that works best for you. When it comes to the number of syllables per line, I tend to try to stick to ten but am more than happy to be a little flexible if the poem flows better as a result. The best test is usually to read it aloud and see how it feels.

First Love and Forever Love – Sonnet Example

Our first love looks quite different to our last,
Our heart is won, completely and in haste,
We'd die for love before much time has passed,
But often these emotions are a waste.

First love so often meets a bitter end,
Hearts won with ease are broken swiftly too.
First lovers rarely graduate to friends,
The love we thought we felt was not quite true.

Last love, true love, is quite a different thing,
We grow together learning how to be,
We start at winter, slowly move to spring,
This love takes time and nurture like a seed,

And like a seed, with time it will grow strong,
Forever binding two hearts that belong.

Form 3: Acrostic

At its simplest, an acrostic is simply a poem where the first letter of each line spells out a word or phrase down the left hand side of the page.

We can challenge ourselves further by writing a double acrostic where both the first and last letters of each line spell out words or phrases or we can combine the acrostic with a different form – so we might write a sonnet that is also an acrostic for example.

Acrostic Format:

Wxxxxx
Oxxxxx
Rxxxxx
Dxxxxx

Double Acrostic Format:

WxxxxxW
OxxxxxO
RxxxxxR
DxxxxxD

Jane – Acrostic Example

Just as things could get no worse
Along came Jane, my wounds to nurse.
Not once did she complain or cry,
Each day she taught me how to fly.

Form 4: Golden Shovel

If you fancy a challenge then a golden shovel is worth a try.

First you need to choose a poem that has inspired you – it's easier if this poem is not too long. It might be a poem you have written yourself or a poem written by someone else that has inspired you in some way. This is Poem A. Your new poem is Poem B.

In order to write Poem B you take Poem A, word by word, and these words form the last word of each line of Poem B – so in reading Poem B, if you just read the last word of each line, you'd effectively be reading Poem A.

Golden Shovel Format:

XXXXXXX If
XXXXXXX you
XXXXXXX read
XXXXXXX these
XXXXXXX words
XXXXXXX you'll
XXXXXXX be
XXXXXXX reading
XXXXXXX poem
XXXXXXX A

And Then There Was You – Golden Shovel Example

There was a time, when
I had not yet met you.
Life was punctuated with a desire to die.
I'm not sure where my head was at.
Never one thought, but 99.
And not one good, back then.
Life was full of people,
But no one to tend
To what was broken, to
Take my hand and to say:
It will be okay…a
Sentiment for which my heart was ripe;
Yet all I did was slowly age.
Before you, life was not good.
But then, a time of new beg-innings
A fresh start, a
Chance to try again at life,
To do it well,
And feel that I had lived.
It almost felt too good, but

Soon, 'I' became 'we'
It turned out, you were all I'd ever wanted…
No more thoughts of dying, each day I want another.
With you, each day is a perfect day.

This was my 200th daily poem and I drew inspiration from my first ever poem 200 days earlier – 'A Ripe Old Age' – if you read the last word of each line of 'And Then There Was You' you'll see the first stanza of 'A Ripe Old Age' which I've included below for reference.

A Ripe Old Age – The Inspiration for My Golden Shovel (My 'Poem A')

When you die at 99,
Then people tend to say:
'A ripe age!'
'Good innings!'
'A life well lived!'
But we wanted another day.

Another day to talk to you,
And laugh at times gone by,
Another day to hold your hand,
It was too soon to say goodbye.

Even in those quiet days,
When your eyes were often closed,
You never ceased from listening,
As you gently dozed…

And as we talked, we learnt a lot
About things that really matter,
As we reviewed a life well spent,
And turned it into chatter.

We hope you found it comforting,
We loved to talk and share,
And as long as we keep talking,
We know you'll still be there.

Form 5: Terza Rima

A Terza Rima is a series of three-line stanzas (called 'tercets') which form a rhyming chain. The middle line of each tercet rhymes with the first and last lines of the subsequent tercet. The lines can be any length though many people choose to use iambic pentameter – ten beats per line.

Your poem can be any length, you just continue repeating in the same pattern. You can finish your poem either with a standalone line or with a rhyming couplet.

Terza Rima Format:

A B A | B C B | C D C | D E D | E (E)

Never Good Enough – Terza Rima Example

You look at me with ill-disguised despair,
Ashamed of what you see before your eyes,
Undressed by your emotion I am bare.

Your body shakes, you're choked with muffled cries.
I hate that I have made you feel this way,
But one day you should try my shoes for size.

You think that if you hope and if you pray,
You'll see return the woman that you love,
But I'm afraid it doesn't work that way.

I don't believe that there's a God above
Nor demons, who know how to steal this pain
That fits me like a much-loved, well-worn glove.

I'm sorry that I've hurt you yet again,
Each time I say I won't but then I do,
You must be tiring fast of this refrain.

I wish that I was good enough for you.

Form 6: Rubáiyát

A Rubáiyát is made up of a series of four-line stanzas (these are called 'quatrains'). In each quatrain, all lines rhyme except the third line. The third line forms the basis for the rhyme in the next quatrain.

You can continue this rhyming pattern for as long as you like. There is no set number of syllables per line.

Rubáiyát Format:

A A B A | B B C B | C C D C | D D E D

'Nana's Wishes' is an example of a Rubáiyát – read it carefully, noting how the rhyme falls. This rhyming pattern can feel quite strange to read if you don't appreciate that you're reading a poem of a specific form. Think about how the rhyming structure adds or detracts from the thoughts and feelings provoked by the poem.

Nana's Wishes – Rubáiyát Example

As soon as I saw her, I knew she would die,
The sight of her old withered limbs made me cry,
She beckoned me over, put on a brave face,
She said she was ready, I thought it a lie.

Please do me a favor, get out of this place,
She said with the palm of her hand on my face,
It'll do you no good, it'll suck out your soul,
So walk out of here now, disappear without trace.

I heard what she said, though it sounded quite droll,
This place was a hungry and giant black hole,
The happiness went out of everyone there,
All of our life and our love this place stole.

I fed her some tea and I brushed her white hair,
And I checked she had toothpaste and clean underwear,
Then I gave her a kiss and with one knowing look,
I left her behind, and a part of me there.

I walked out forever, the courage it took,
To obey her strange wishes should not be mistook
For someone uncaring who just stayed away
So as she withered they'd not have to look.

I wanted to visit my Nana each day,
My heart said: Oh Nana don't send me away,
But she wanted me gone and she wanted me strong,
Because she knew soon that there would come a day.

When the grief of her passing would be our new song,
And she knew that it needed somebody quite strong,
To help all the others to handle their grief,
The day after I left, Nana sang her last song.

Form 7: Anaphora

Anaphora is a technique where a word or phrase is repeatedly used to start lines within your poem. You can be fairly flexible in how you approach this technique. Below is a poem I wrote to my daughter using Anaphora.

Everything Changed – Anaphora Example

Everything changed when we learnt of you,
When we found out we'd be three, not two.
Everything changed as my belly grew,
As we quickly fell in love with you.

Everything changed the moment you arrived,
Blinking, wrinkled, very much alive.
Everything changed, we were parents now.
We'd read the books, but we weren't sure how.

Everything changed when you learned to smile,
Sleepless nights and nappies all seemed worthwhile,
Everything changed as we learnt the ropes,
Gaining skills and scars and dreams and hopes.

Everything changed when I first said goodbye,
Just for an hour – but it made me cry.
Everything changed when you learned to walk,
Things changed yet more when you learned to talk.

Everything's changing almost every day,
But we wouldn't want it any other way.
Everything changes as you teach us how to live,
With all the love and laughter you so freely give.

Form 8: Pyramid

This is a very simple technique where you vary the length of the lines of your poem so that it forms a pyramid or triangle on the page. You can create a horizontal pyramid with shorter lines towards the beginning and end of the poem and the longest lines in the middle and left justifying.

Horizontal Pyramid Format:

Xxx
Xxx xxx
Xxx xxx xxx
Xxx xxx
Xxx

You can achieve a vertical pyramid by writing increasingly long lines and centre justifying your final poem.

Vertical Pyramid Format:

Xxx
Xxx xxx
Xxx xxx xxx
Xxx xxx xxx xxx
Xxx xxx xxx xxx xxx
Xxx xxx xxx xxx xxx xxx

Your poem can be of any length and rhythm.

You can add to the challenge by including a specific number of words or syllables in each line, but often the final visual effect is most pleasing if you consider how the poem looks on the page rather than adhering to rigid rules about length.

Once you have tried playing around with form on the page like this, you might be tempted to play with other shapes – go with it! As you write your poem, think both about the words and the sense of the poem but also about how its form on the page will encourage a reader to interpret it in a certain way.

In the poem 'Anorexia' I played with the pyramid form to convey the idea of weight gain and loss by the lengthening and shortening of the lines. In the first half of the poem I imagined everyone around me willing me to eat and gain weight – so the lines got longer, fatter. In the second half of the poem, I recognised my urge to continue to lose weight, and I tried to demonstrate this through increasingly short, thin lines.

Anorexia – Pyramid Example

It'll kill you.
They told me.
I couldn't care less.
The thing that I knew,
But I could not confess,
Was that unless it killed me,
Then I'd always know,
That there'd been,
Just a little bit,
Further
To Go.

Poetry prompts

Sometimes we may have a desire to try our hand at poetry writing but we're not sure where to start. Or maybe we're a little more accomplished but we're lacking inspiration. If that happens, using a prompt to spur creativity can be really helpful. These prompts are designed to inspire rather than restrict so feel free to adapt them and run with them as feels appropriate. You can mix the prompts with the formats in the previous section if you want an extra challenge.

You can also collect your own prompts by saving images or phrases that especially appeal to you throughout the week and use them as a starting point for a poem. Almost anything can act as a prompt – it just needs to provide a hook to get the creative process started.

There is a wide range of prompt types in the following pages and I've included an example poem with every prompt – an interesting follow up can be to explore the different ways of responding to the prompt by comparing and contrasting my approach with yours. There is no right or wrong way to respond to a prompt and you might choose to respond to the same prompt several times if it especially resonates or you want a chance to experiment with different poetic forms or techniques.

Prompt 1: Dear me…

Write a poem giving advice to your younger self. You might choose a relatively recent you or you may go back several years – decide which version of you you'd like to write your poem to before you start.

You might like to consider:

- What do you know now that you didn't know then?

- What worried you unnecessarily?

- What misconceptions did you have?

- What did you think the future held?

- What bad advice did you follow that you shouldn't have?

—— Dear Me – A Poem to My Teenage Self

No one cares
If you're fat or thin.
You do not need
To starve, to win.
One day,
You will understand,
As children grip
Your loving hand,
Your body isn't yours
To use,
To torment, hate
And to abuse.
Your body's
Worth much more
Than that.
In time,
You'll learn
To love the fat,
That shows you grew
A child inside,
And shows you nursed her.
You'll feel pride
About your arms,
So long and strong,
That cuddle children
All day long;
And legs
Which one day carry you

Twenty-six point bloody two
Miles – straight into the arms,
Of those who call you
Wife and Mum.
They love you
If you're fat,
Or thin.
You do not need
To starve, to win.

Prompt 2: Something that scares you

Write a poem about something that scares you.

You might like to consider:

- Should your poem be literal (e.g. snakes) or more abstract (e.g. public speaking)?

- Why does what you've chosen scare you?

- How does it make you feel?

- Would you like to overcome your fear?

- What would change if you did overcome your fear?

- Does your fear stop you doing things/change how you approach things?

— Please Keep Waking

I'm scared that one day
When I wake,
You won't be there,
That death will take
You from my life,
Steal you away…
I couldn't bear
A single day,
Without you sat
Right by my side,
Without the hope
That you provide,
Without the love
I feel so deep.
So please,
Keep waking
From your sleep.

Prompt 3: Confusing figure of speech

Write a poem inspired by a figure of speech that is used commonly in your country but could easily be misunderstood by a foreigner, or a child.

I live in London so I could consider using the following idioms:

- Raining cats and dogs

- Get on like a house on fire

- The cat's got your tongue

- Chew the fat

- All talk, no trousers.

You get the idea. You can take any approach to your poem that you like, but it might help you to think about:

- What does the phrase you've chosen mean?

- What might people *think* it means?

- Why did you choose this particular phrase?

- Do you remember the first time you heard it or being confused by it as a kid?

- Should your poem explain or explore the phrase or just use it in passing?

- Should your poem use the phrase at all or just allude to it?

- Should your poem tell the story of a misunderstanding based on your phrase?

- Should your poem include one or several idioms/phrases?

—— Itchy Feet

My mum has got this problem,
That the doc can't seem to treat.
It's a tickly scratchy problem,
It's a problem with her feet.

She tells me that they're itchy,
And the itch won't seem to go;
I've tried to help by scratching
Both her soles and all her toes.

The scratching doesn't seem to help,
I don't know what to do.
Dad says the answer may be found
In Prague or Kathmandu…

Prompt 4: A Haiku from your window

Write a Haiku inspired by what you can see from the nearest window to you right now.

You might think Haiku are easy because they're short…well they're short, but I'm not sure they're easy – they are good fun to experiment with though. There is guidance about how to write a Haiku in the chapter about poetic forms.

You might like to consider:

- Do you want to stick to the traditional format and content of Haiku or are you happy to be more flexible?

- What can you see from your window – what jumps out at you?

- What are the small details you can see from your window that might often go unnoticed?

- Is your view one you're very familiar with? Does it change with the seasons?

- What feelings do you want to evoke with your Haiku?

—— *Sunset*

Colour explosion
As the sun departs once more.
The day is ending.

Prompt 5: The last line changes everything

Write a poem where the last line changes the way the whole poem is perceived. You might like to consider:

- What is your poem about/what do you want your reader to misinterpret it as being about?

- Read your poem bearing both meanings in mind to make sure the illusion is complete.

- Should you mislead the reader until the last line?

- Or should the meaning just remain unclear until the end?

- How could you lead your reader to understand your words in two ways?

- How can you ensure the last line makes the true meaning clear?

Watch Over Them

He loved to watch the children play,
Their endless smiles made his day,
Their joy and laughter, come what may,
Made all his sadness go away.
He loved to watch the children play,
Then on those children he would prey.

Prompt 6: An unlikely thank you

Write a poem of thanks to someone you know or have encountered who would be surprised by your gratitude. This might be because they are not used to being thanked (the man who delivers your groceries so swiftly and courteously each week) or because they do not realise how grateful you are to them (your sister who always picks you up when you're down).

You might like to consider:

- Who is your poem for – what is special about them?

- Why are you thanking them?

- Should you talk in general terms about your gratitude or is there a specific incident you wish to draw on?

- How do you think that person felt when carrying out the deed for which you are grateful?

- Do you think this person does similar things for other people?

- What sets this person apart from others doing a similar role/with whom you have a similar relationship?

- Do you think there are others that would want to join you in your thanks? Who? Why?

- How do you think this poem will make the person you are thanking feel?

— To My Godmother

I never stop to thank you,
Though I know I really should,
You're one of those few people who
Convince me life is good.

You haven't had it easy,
But I don't hear you complain.
Even at your most unwell,
You didn't talk of pain.

Instead you thought of others,
It has always been your way,
To put the rest before yourself,
Day, after day, after day.

The only thing you asked me
Between your bouts of radiation,
Was that I should send you photos
To act as recovery inspiration.

And so I sent them daily,
All these photos of my girls.
They seemed quite unremarkable.
You watched their lives unfurl.

You took those pictures everywhere
Boring nurses and friends too,
It made me learn the power,
That love has to see us through.

You're doing rather better now,
But still enjoy our snaps
(And I feel rather guilty
If I let my picture taking lapse)

Now I have a record
Of two perfect little girls.
Thanks to you, over the years
I'll re-watch their lives unfurl.

Thanks too for the support you give,
The strength you help me find.
You're a very special person,
Without doubt, one of a kind.

Prompt 7: An antidote to nightmares

Write a poem designed to help somebody (or yourself) to overcome their nightmares.

You might like to consider:

- Who is the nightmare sufferer? An adult? A child? You?

- What is the nightmare about?

- How might you be able to soothe using your words or rhythm?

A Lullaby to Ward off Nightmares

Hush little darling, dry your tears,
Mummy's here to calm your fears,
To make the monsters go away,
To make night feel as safe as day,
To hold you close, cuddle you tight,
Until you're calm and feel no fright.
Open your eyes and look around,
Plonk your feet on steady ground,
There's nothing here to fear, my love,
No monsters lurking up above
The wardrobe, nor beneath your bed,
The monsters all lurk in your head.
You can make them go away,
Or make them friends with whom to play;
Imagine them in silly clothes,
Or with a feather up their nose,
Or with big shoes or silly hair,
Or wearing baggy underwear!
And soon you'll see that they're not scary,
(Even though they're big and hairy)
Now your foes are friends, my dear
Please sleep softly, without fear.

Prompt 8: First phrase, last phrase
Write a poem in which the first phrase is also the last phrase.
You might like to consider:

- Should you use the phrase just twice or elsewhere in the poem too – if so, where?
- Should you choose a phrase with multiple meanings or just one?
- Should the repetition of the phrase be integral to your poem or almost coincidental?
- Should you use a long or short phrase?
- Should the phrase make up a whole line, or part of a line?
- Should the phrase have the same meaning in the first line and last line?

— The End?

It's not the end,
It's the beginning.
He told her
As he signed her release forms,
Declared her 'sane'
And sent her gaily
Into the big wide world.
She wasn't ready.
She'd tried to tell him.
The world was not exciting
It was terrifying.
A place that made no sense
And made her hurt
In ways she could not explain.
She had a plan.
All it would take
Was two dozen pain killers.
She quelled her rising panic,
As she walked
Hesitantly
From the ward,
By reminding herself:
It's not the beginning,
It's the end.

Prompt 9: Open with a question

Write a poem that opens with a question.

You might like to consider:

- Who is asking the question?

- Is the question actual or rhetorical?

- Should your poem attempt to answer the question?

- Should you ask further questions in your poem?

- Could the question be interpreted in more than one way?

- Should the poem take the form of a conversation?

- Should the poem ask a question or questions of the reader?

Like Father, Like Son

Why did you do it?
Said mother to son
She waved her fist angrily,
Palming the gun.
I don't know.
He told her,
Ashamed of the way
That things had conspired
Against him that day.
This wasn't the way
It was supposed to be,
Uttered the mother,
Can you not see,
That if you'd just waited
A little more time,
Away we'd have run
And now things would be fine.
The car, it was coming,
Help was on its way
But look at this mess
Now there's really no way.
Let's dispose of the body!
Said the boy filled with hope
I don't think, said his mother,
That my nerves could cope
With the shifting of bodies
And the feeling of sin.
There's nothing left for it

We'll turn ourselves in.
You shouldn't have shot him
But now that it's done
We'll just have to live
With the fact that we're scum.
She broke down in tears,
She was sad as could be,
Small crime was one thing
But now she could see
That her son wasn't like her,
He did not draw the line,
At jewels and money
And things posh and fine.
He took things much further,
That much she now knew,
And she knew in her heart of hearts
What to do.
She picked up the gun
And she loaded it twice
And shot once in the air
(The thrill was quite nice)
The sound shocked her son
And he turned round to see
She had the gun pointed
Directly at he.
She shot it and wept
At the fear in his eyes,
But she knew that the world
Would prefer that he die.
She was certain that now he had
Tasted first blood,
That no one was safe,
That his small mind would flood
With desire and hatred,
Of his fellow man,
And he'd kill and he'd kill
And it would be worse than
This one single shot,
Which she put through his head.
She knew in her heart
He was better off dead.

Prompt 10: The street where you grew up

Write a poem set in the street where you grew up.

You might like to consider:

- Should the poem be about your childhood or just use the street as a setting?
- How do you think the street may have changed since you were a child?
- What was interesting or special about the street where you grew up?
- Were there any interesting people or places in your street you could draw on in your poem?
- Do you have any special memories of your street you'd like to write about?
- Did you like the street where you grew up? Why?
- What did your street smell like or sound like?
- What did other people think about your street when you were a child?

Slade Gang

When I think back to my younger days,
On Slade Road, Ilfracombe
And recall many times gone by,
Only happy memories loom.
It was a rather special place,
Where I made lifelong friends,
We now live many miles apart,
But friendship never ends.
We were young adventurers,
Who were often stuck up trees,
Or running home for plasters
For our newly bloodied knees.
We were fishermen as well some days,
We loved to tickle trout,
And the shy and tiny minnows too,
When we could coax them out.
We made mud pies and rode our bikes
And sometimes sledges too,
We were a very happy gang
Never short of things to do.
The Slade Gang was amazing,
And as I think about it now,
I realise how blessed I was
To have such special pals.

Prompt 11: Light and dark

Write a poem that features both light and dark.

You might like to consider:

- What kind of light and dark should you consider, for example day and night, different moods, skin colour?

- Could you consider more than one type of light and dark in your poem?

- Should you major on the light and dark theme or just use it to complement your poem?

- Should you draw on other contrasts too or just light and dark?

- Could the way you present your poem (e.g. bold font vs italics) be used to emphasise your message?

- Should you draw comparisons between light and dark or leave your reader to interpret your meaning?

—— Chink of Light

Life was getting darker,
Feeling bleaker by the day.
He couldn't really manage,
He had truly lost his way.
He thought he'd like to end it all,
Make the pain all go away.
He couldn't face the darkness,
Of another failed day.
Then a friend came up and asked him
How are things, are you okay?
And he nearly didn't answer,
But his mood began to sway.
He saw the smallest chink of light,
He saw it in the way,
That his friend had held her hand out,
As she asked about his day.
He heard it in the way she clearly meant
Are you okay?
Not another platitude,
Not something just to say.
He could tell she really meant it,
So he found the guts to say:
Thanks so much for asking,
But in fact, I'm not okay.

She listened and she held him,
On this dark and failing day.
And as he poured his heart out
He found his problems didn't weigh
Quite so heavy on his heart now
And he thought he saw a way,
That he could make it to the end
Of this most dark and dismal day.

Prompt 12: No punctuation
Write a poem which features no punctuation other than line breaks.
    You might like to consider:

- How can you use line breaks in lieu of all other punctuation?

- Can you help to punctuate your poem by how it is formatted on the page?

- What part does punctuation usually play in your poetry? What happens if you just remove it unthinkingly?

- Is there a clever way to replace punctuation – e.g. could we write it in as we might in an old fashioned telegram?

- Can you use the lack of punctuation to make your poem special?

- Should you draw attention to the lack of punctuation or attempt to hide it?

Headlong in Love

everything was moving so fast
she had found her true love now at last
she loved him and he loved her back
did it matter so much he was black
could those divisions not live in the past

not to her did it matter at all
the issue of colour was small
but her parents forbid it
so for weeks they both hid it
and they set themselves up for a fall

for true love does not like to be hidden
and it grows and it morphs quite unbidden
then it chews you and spits you
and batters and hits you
until you do what is forbidden

they soon ran away hand in hand
in the search of less prejudiced land
but their parents chased after
it led to disaster
and did not end how they both planned

they died hand in hand with each other
at the hand of the young girl's big brother
despite making a pact
he could not live with his act
and the family soon lost another

Prompt 13: Describe a smell

Write a poem which describes the smell of something.

You might like to consider:

- Should the whole poem focus on describing a smell or should that just form part of the poem?

- Should you describe one smell or many?

- What feelings should you try to evoke with your descriptions of smell?

- Should you describe the same smell from multiple viewpoints (smellpoints?!)?

- What is unique or special about the particular smell you have in mind?

- How can the use of smell contribute to the feelings your poem evokes?

- Should you choose a smell that is very familiar or try to describe a more alien smell to your readers?

—— Roses

Their scent hitchhiked on the breeze,
Tantalising the nostrils of all who passed.
Delicate notes of summer days,
Sweet drops of beautiful
Picking up where the scent of grass clippings left off.
Filling the void left by giddy summer thoughts,
And bringing a smile to the face
Of all who smelt them.
In full bloom, the roses' beauty was unparalleled,
Yet their looks paled in comparison to their scent.
A woman passed, doubling back
To consume the heady smell.
She was reminded of the months she carried her first child,
When she felt intoxicated by the smell of roses.
She breathed deeply.
The floral notes robust, yet delicate, filled her completely.
One hand held a rose to her face,
The other gently touched her stomach.
Flat and empty.
She realised she was broody.
It was time.

Prompt 14: The meaning of life

Write a poem which explores or explains the meaning of life.

You might like to consider:

- What is the meaning of life from your point of view, and from the point of view of others?

- Whose viewpoint should the poem be written from?

- Who is your intended audience? Adults? Children?

- Should you try to be humorous?

- Should you present one or multiple viewpoints in your poem?

- Should you explore the meaning of life, explain it, or both?

- Should your poem raise questions or answer them or both?

- What kind of response might you hope to evoke from your readers?

Life is
A series of moments,
Those moments
A long line of gifts,
Those gifts are there
For the unwrapping;
Some treasures,
Some tragic,
All gifts?

Prompt 15: School days

Write a poem which explores the adage that your school days are the best days of your life.

You might like to consider:

- Do you think that your school days are the best days of your life? Why?

- Should you write a poem based on the premise that the adage is untrue?

- Should you draw on your own experiences or write more generally?

- Are there any especially vivid recollections you can draw on/adapt?

- Do you think it's easier being at school now or back when you were a child?

- What is your best memory of school?

- What was the hardest thing about being at school?

- What would the perfect school experience have looked like?

—— School Days

As his father told him,
Again,
That these were the best days,
He tried to smile.
He tried to hide the fear,
And sadness.
To resist the urge to cry.
If these were the best days,
He thought,
Then what was the point?
Why go on?
Can you go downhill
When you're already
In a valley of despair?
Later,
As he was punched
And spat at,
Laughed at
And ridiculed,
His father's words echoed
In his mind.
The best days?
Perhaps
The worst was yet to come.

Prompt 16: A set of instructions

Write a poem which provides a series of instructions about how to do something. You might like to consider:

- Should you try to make something unexciting poetic, for example how to make a marble cake, or should you take a looser approach to the brief and provide instructions on how to live a happy life, for instance?

- How detailed should your instructions be?

- Should you choose something you're familiar with, or learn about something new as you're writing your poem?

- Should you use an existing set of instructions as the basis for your poem?

- Should you try to make your instructions accurate so they could be followed or is this unimportant to you?

- Should you try to inject sarcasm or humour by using particular viewpoints when writing your instructions?

— A Recipe for Happy Children

Take one puppy,
He must be small
He mustn't nip
Or bite at all.
Take him home,
And when you're there,
Let the children
Take good care
Of their new friend,
Who's slightly sad,
But kisses and cuddles,
Make him feel less bad.
Set some rules,
Just one or two,
So the kids
Know what to do.
Then sit right back
With your feet up,
And watch the kids
Enjoy their pup.

Prompt 17: Admiration acrostic

Write a poem in which the first letter of every line spells out the name of somebody you admire and the poem explains why you admire them.

You might like to consider:

- Should you just use a first name or a last name too to give you more lines?
- Should you choose someone you know or somebody famous?
- What do you most admire about the person you've chosen? It might help to brainstorm possible reasons before trying to fit them into your poem.
- Should your poem have a particular rhyme or rhythm to it?

If you are feeling very ambitious you could also spell out something of your choice with the last letter of each line too.

Just as things could get no worse
Along came Jane, my wounds to nurse.
Not once did she complain or cry,
Each day she taught me how to fly.

Prompt 18: Rhyme and reason

Write a poem which uses rhyme to communicate a serious topic in a light-hearted way.

You might like to consider:

- What serious topic should you approach – is there something you feel strongly about?
- How can you incorporate rhyme without seeming to belittle your serious message?
- How can you use rhyme to help you to make your point?
- Should you use rhyme throughout or just in places to emphasise a point?
- What type of rhyming scheme should you use?
- Should you use a regular rhythm to emphasise your rhyme or go for something more subtle?

You Never Lived Inside my Tummy

You never lived inside my tummy,
But that makes me no less your Mummy,
I love you still, with all my heart,
Despite your slightly different start.

I couldn't wait to see your face,
To feel that first, unsure, embrace.
You didn't grow inside of me,
But now you are a part of me.

And part of me, you'll always stay,
And no, the start won't go away,
But please remember, from the start,
You weren't my flesh, you are my heart.

Prompt 19: How we met

Write a poem which tells the story of how you met your best friend or partner. You might like to consider:

- Who are the people you could possibly write about?

- Would you be able to write a better poem based on the most interesting person in the list above, or the person you met under the most interesting circumstances?

- Should you focus solely on how and when you met or go on to tell the story of your relationship?

- What makes your relationship special with the person you've chosen?

- What might have happened slightly differently that day to have stopped you meeting?

- How would your life be different if you had not met?

- What did you think of the person you've chosen in the first moments you spent with them?

- What did you think they thought of you?

—— Nice is Good

I knew when we met
There was no going back
He's too nice! I protested
His life is on track.
You certainly weren't
Like the others I'd known
Whose strange kind of love
I had so soon outgrown.
You were friendly and charming
Clever and cute
I distinctly recall
That I couldn't compute
What a boy like yourself
Saw in little old me,
But you said you saw something
And taught me to see.
The first time I met you
Was almost the last,
But a small voice inside me
Was simply aghast…

You mustn't desert him
Because he's too nice,
(The small voice inside me
Gave quite sage advice)
And I'm glad that I listened
Because 11 years on,
You're still nice, but my
Past reservations are gone.
And I think nice is good,
I think nice is the best,
And our lifetime together,
Is a fabulous quest.

Prompt 20: Strip tease

Write a poem in which someone takes their clothes off for an unusual reason.
You might like to consider:

- Should you tell a real story or an imagined one?

- Who is going to take their clothes off and why?

- What are they wearing?

- Are they going to remove their clothes or will they be removed by someone or something else?

- Should your poem be funny or serious?

- Should the undressing be a central part of your poem or not?

- Could the undressing form part of a series of strange events?

- Should you consider a metaphorical undressing (e.g. your protagonist could bare their emotions rather than their body) either alongside or instead of a physical undressing?

—— Wobbly Bits

She'd been a little short of cash,
And saw the advert, feeling rash
She'd called the number,
Volunteered.
It was as strange
As she had feared.
The students came in twos and threes,
Here to paint her knocking knees,
And curly hair
And wobbly bits,
And great big, sagging, ageing tits.
We're ready.
Said the lecturer,
Who really had been kind to her.
He'd fed her biscuits,
Poured her tea,
Made sure she had been for a wee.
But now the time had come at last,
Where she must bare her bottom (vast)
And step out of her pantyhose,
And put her body out on show.
She slipped away behind a screen,
So her undressing went unseen,

So no one saw her slip and fumble,
No one heard her quietly mumble
Why oh why… Why am I here?
Her stomach tied in knots of fear.
She undressed quickly as she could,
Before she knew it, there she stood,
As naked as her day of birth,
Expecting giggles, fits of mirth.
But as she sat astride the chair,
Self-consciously smoothing her grey hair.
No one laughed or raised a smile
They simply sat and stared a while,
Then lifted pens, or a well-worn brush,
And slowly she could feel the flush
Of horror that had scarred her face,
Retreating, gone, without a trace.
She realised soon, that as their muse,
She had no dignity to lose.
She was just knees and arms and tits.
They liked to sketch her wobbly bits.
They thought her interesting, not old,
And loved the stories told by folds.
The grey hairs and the pocks and marks,
Each one, a perfect work of art.
They loved her, and they let her know
By putting on a public show.
She bought a piece, and now her face,
Sits just above her fireplace.

Prompt 21: Love is…

Write a poem which explains the meaning of love to a child.

You might like to consider:

- What is love?

- How can you simplify this concept to make it understood by a child?

- Should your poem be purely explanatory or a story to demonstrate love?

- Why is it important that a child understands what love is?

- What examples could you use to explain what love is?

- What examples could you use to demonstrate what love is not?

- What was your understanding of love as a child?

— *Love Is*

Love is when you feel safe
All snuggled in my arms.
Love is when you know that I'll
Protect you from all harm.
Because of love you know
That there is nothing I won't do
For a certain little girl,
Yes, of course, I mean you!
Love will give you courage,
And love will make you brave.
Love will grow you memories
You'll always want to save.
Love will make you feel content,
And ready to explore,
Love is never ending,
With true love, there's always more.

Prompt 22: One word title

Write a poem which has a one word title. Include the word used for the title at least twice in the body of the poem.

You might like to consider:

- What would be the best word to use? For example, a name, a place, an exclamation.

- How can you use the repetition of the word to add meaning to your poem?

- When repeated should the word have the same meaning as in the title or should you use a word with multiple meanings?

- Where in your poem should you repeat the title word? Will the positioning of your repetition affect the mood or meaning of your poem?

— Regret

Regret leaves such a bitter taste
That lingers, foul and sour.
A taste that comes to haunt you
Day by day and hour by hour.

Regret is best avoided,
At all costs, if possible,
Because it takes the nicest folk
And turns them most horrible.

Regret makes us look backwards,
With our twenty-twenty eyes,
And pinpoint a decision,
Once thought sound, but now despised.

Regret is never helpful,
And it never paves the way,
For a life that's full and happy
Where we cherish every day.

So let's take regret and throw it
In a big pit with despair,
And hatred and with cruelty
And let them fester there.

Prompt 23: Fragile friendships

Write a poem which considers the fragility of friendship.

You might like to consider:

- What kind of friendships should you consider – childhood/adult etc.?
- Do you think friendships are fragile or not?
- Is there a particular friendship that could inspire your writing?
- Why are friendships important?
- What happens when they don't work out?
- How can you strengthen a fragile friendship?

—— Fragile Friendships

What happens when
You know someone,
But what you knew was wrong?
That what you were
Told was the truth,
Was pure lies all along?
It's hard to move on forwards,
To forgive and to forget.
Friendships built on trust and love,
From the first day that you met,
Are vulnerable to change of heart
Or lies that once weren't told.
Friendships built on cracks and lies
Will never grow that old.
It's tempting not to tell the truth,
If you have things to hide,
But the day you lose
The friend you had,
You'll wish you never lied.

_____

Prompt 24: Extended metaphor

Write a poem which is an extended metaphor

You might like to consider:

- Is there a metaphor you've used in other writing that you could expand for this poem?

- Should your poem be amusing or serious?

- Should you use a well-rehearsed metaphor or explore something new?

- Should you use one metaphor or more?

- Could you (should you?) contain metaphors within your metaphor?

— Blanket of Snow

It was dark,
It was cold,
It was winter.
She woke from troubled dreams,
Of monsters and corridors.
It had been a tossing
And turning
Kind of night.
So imagine her delight
When she peeked outside
To see a blanket of snow.
A blanket with an eerie
Early morning glow.
Her family slept,
So out she crept,
To the snow.
The blanket stretched for miles,
Lumps and bumps marked places,
Where shrubs and flowers
Hid their faces.
The blanket was perfect.
No holes.
No creases.
Perfectly laundered,
White as…
Snow.
Soon it would go.
Of that she was sure,
So for now,

She danced and twirled,
Sashayed and swirled,
In this perfect blanket,
Which warmed her.
From the inside,
Out.

Prompt 25: Your 100th birthday

Write a poem which could be read at your own 100th birthday.

You might like to consider:

- What would you like people to think of you when you're 100?

- What life events might be highlighted in such a poem (some may already have happened, some will be in the future)?

- Would you prefer a fun poem or a serious one?

- Who else should feature in your poem?

- What kind of party could you imagine yourself having aged 100?

- Whose voice should your poem be told by?

Hope for One Hundred

She's done this
And done that
And the other.
She's a wife
And a mum
And grandmother.
She's learned stuff,
And taught stuff,
And wrote
Even more stuff,
And she's currently
Writing another.
But none of that matters,
Not really,
She's world famous,
Of course,
Or quite nearly,
But above all you'll find,
She's incredibly kind,
And she listens,
And gives her love freely.

Prompt 26: Time difference

Write a poem which features a time difference.

You might like to consider:

- Which countries are concerned?

- How big is the time difference?

- Is the time difference a central or peripheral theme?

- Could the time difference lead to an amusing incident or misunderstanding?

Man and Boy

I'm you,
From the future
Said the man
To the boy.
And the boy couldn't help
But feel
Somewhat coy.
If the story
This weathered old man
Told was true
Then imagine
The things
He had seen
And he knew.
But it couldn't be true.
Prove it!
Challenged the boy.
And now, not the boy,
But the man,
Became coy.
On your left little toe,
There's a nasty red mark,
That you got
When you tripped
As you weed in the dark,
And your Mum
Calls you pumpkin,
You don't like blue cheese,
And you're ever so
Madly in love
With Louise.
But could it be true?

Just how could it be so?
Said the boy to the man
Who just shrugged
I don't know…
But it's lovely to see you,
To see me, I mean.
And they looked at each other
And each wiped his face clean,
And then brushed back his hair
With a right-handed flick,
And gave his snub nose
A surreptitious, quick pick.
Similarities uncanny,
They soon turned their mind
To consider what differences
Between them they'd find.
Well the man was quite old
And quite weathered and worn,
Whilst the boy was quite young,
Hair untidily shorn.
The old man had seen
Quite a lot of the world,
He was jaded,
Dreams faded,
The young boy
Not so.
For adventure
And travels and fun
Filled his thoughts,
And in his spare time
He got up to
All sorts,
Whilst the old man preferred
To relax and recline,
And read a good book
Whilst he supped a fine wine.
But the more time
They spent
With each other,
The more,
Both the man
And the boy
Of one thing,
Became sure,
That despite the differences,
There couldn't be more,
That this self-seeded friendship
Would surely endure.

Prompt 27: Screensaver

Write a poem which is inspired by the current screensaver on your phone or computer.

You might like to consider:

- When was the picture taken and who by?

- Why did you choose it as your screensaver?

- How does that picture make you feel?

- What was happening when it was taken?

- Who or what is in it?

— Tap-Tap-Tap

Head down, focused,
Tap-Tap-Tap.
Must keep working,
No time to nap.
Rain hits the window
Tap-Tap-Tap.
Mustn't get distracted
By the slip slop slap.
Thinking, typing,
Tap-Tap-Tap.
Deadlines bringing on
A stressed out flap,
'Til fists knock the door with a
Tap-Tap-Tap.
Mum it's time for stories
And snuggles on your lap.
Girls with brollies poke me,
Tap-Tap-Tap.
Time to stop work,
Shut the laptop. Snap.

Prompt 28: Apology

Write a poem which makes an apology you've always regretted not making.

You might like to consider:

- What do you wish to apologise for?
- Who are you apologising to?
- Why did you not apologise at the time?
- Why have you not apologised since?
- Do you think your lack of apology was noted?
- How did the situation for which you never apologised impact on you or others?

—— *I'm Sorry*

I'm sorry.
I wasn't lying.
I wasn't.
You were the only person to whom I told the truth.
The only one I trusted.
I told no one else,
And so you thought I'd lied.
To you.
Lied to you – how could I?
You wore your disappointment on your face.
Why didn't I explain?
Or apologise?
So many times I almost did,
Words on the tip of my tongue.
But the moment was never right.
The scar not ready to be poked.
I thought there would be more time.
I was wrong.
You're gone,
And...
I'm sorry.

Prompt 29: Simple pleasures

Write a poem which celebrates a simple pleasure in life (e.g. clean bed linen).
You might like to consider:

- What pleasure would you like to celebrate?

- When did you last experience that pleasure?

- What about it makes it feel special?

- Should you encourage others to experience this pleasure via your words?

- How did you learn about this pleasure – who taught you and how?

—— *Hugs*

Strong arms looped
Around a weary body,
Holding it up
And hugging the hard day out,
Is one of the little things
That make life okay.
As those arms hold me tight,
I know that just everything
Will be alright.

Prompt 30: Twelve lines long

Write a poem which is twelve lines long.

You might like to consider:

- What should be the topic of your poem?
- How can you convey what you want to say in so few lines?
- How long should each line be?
- Should your poem rhyme?
- Have you read poems of a similar length that you've enjoyed?

—— *Manifesto*

Propaganda in their pockets,
And horror in their hearts,
Instantly they realised that
This is the way war starts.
A harmless little flyer,
And a chance to speak your mind,
Can become a moment when
The blind will lead the blind.
Taking leaflets from their pockets,
They burned them in a fire,
So they couldn't warp the minds
They were intended to inspire.

Prompt 31: Doors

Write a poem which features the opening and closing of doors.

You might like to consider:

- Should your doors be literal or metaphorical or both?

- Should the doors symbolise something? What?

- Should the doors form the major part of your poem or be incidental?

- How can you use rhyme, rhythm and your choice of words to emphasise the opening and closing of doors?

- Should you consider one set of doors or multiple?

—— Bathroom fun

Quickly!
Shouted Ellie,
As she opened up the door.
If you don't come fast
Then Mum will come
And make us wash the floor.
The floor was quite delightfully,
Drenched in suds and foam,
Lyra hurried through the door
To make a soap-filled home.
Ellie slammed the door shut,
In the hope their Mum would stay
Far off from the bathroom,
And that they'd have time to play,
In the world they had created,
That was magical and soapy,
They laughed and squealed,
And slid about,
Both acting rather dopey.
When the door was opened
By their frazzled looking Mum,
The girls both hung their heads low
As she'd come to stop their fun.
Her eyes flashed blue with anger,
For a moment, then she smiled,
And told the girls that if they must
They could play here for a while.
They promised they would tidy up
The bath, the walls and floor.
And so their Mum left them to play
And gently, shut the door.

Prompt 32: Favorite colour

Write a poem which features your favourite colour throughout.

You might like to consider:

- What is your favorite colour and why?

- Should you mention the colour by name or just refer to things that are that colour?

- How often should you refer to the colour?

- How can you use your favorite colour to paint vivid imagery with your words?

- What mood does your favorite colour evoke? Should your poem reflect that?

- Should you include other colours too?

The Colour Purple

It was strangely beautiful,
The way the middle,
Almost black,
Faded to a lighter purple
By degrees.
Lines of red,
Green
And blue
Ran through,
But purple dominated.
A beautiful colour.
It made her think of chocolate,
Smooth and creamy,
Luxurious in its shiny purple wrappers.
It made her think of royalty,
Adorned with diamonds,
Kept warm in purple cloaks.
It made her think of knuckles,
Swollen, broken, purple,
A perfect match,
For her ugly,
Beautiful,
Broken
Face.

Prompt 33: Good news

Write a poem which celebrates good news you have recently heard.
You might like to consider:

- What is the news?

- How did you hear it?

- Why is it good news?

- Will it impact on you or others? How?

- How can you strike a celebratory tone with your words?

—— *Good News*

Good news,
She says.
It's gone.
We don't speak,
But share a moment.
A moment of memories
Of chemo,
And vomiting,
And hair loss,
And pain.
But now,
It's gone.
She can reclaim
Her life again.
Good news.

Prompt 34: Life lesson

Write a poem which is inspired by the most important lesson that you've ever learned

You might like to consider:

- What is the most important lesson you've ever learned?

- Who taught it to you?

- How did they teach it to you?

- How has it impacted you?

- Did you realise its import right away? If not then, when?

— A Lesson in Failure

There was a time
When I was paralysed
With fear.
Fear of failure.
What would people think,
I thought,
If I tried,
But did not succeed?
It seemed almost better
Not to try at all.
If you do not try,
You cannot fail,
Thought my younger self.
Not so,
You said,
Your next words
Remain with me always:
It is only when you do not try,
That you truly fail.
And so,
I try.

_____

Prompt 35: New beginning

Write a poem which is about a new beginning
You might like to consider:

- Why is there a need for a new beginning?

- What does it look like?

- Can you draw on inspiration from your own history or imagined future?

- What are the benefits of a fresh start?

- What must we leave behind when we start again?

A New Beginning

The sadness induced
As the last page is turned
Of a novel
That has absorbed,
Enthralled,
Delighted
And intrigued,
Is matched only
By the eager anticipation
Afforded by a virgin paperback;
Spine unbroken,
Pages unturned,
Story, as yet, unfurled.
A new beginning.

Prompt 36: Reprimand

Write a poem in which someone is reprimanded.

You might like to consider:

- Is there someone or something you would like to tell off?

- Could you draw on your own experiences or those of a friend?

- How can you strike a tone which adequately captures the seriousness (or otherwise) of the reprimand?

- In what way is the person reprimanded?

- Is it fair?

- What is their response?

— Mum Can't Win

You're always making my life hard Mum
Why do I have to wipe my bum?
Please don't make me brush my teeth
Or comb my hair or eat my beef.
Why's my favourite dress not clean?
Not twenty beans, I want fifteen.
Please not that knife and not that fork,
Don't you listen when I talk?
I like the green one…not that green,
The green that has a bluey sheen.
Where's my doll mum? Is it lost?
Why'd you lose it? Now I'm cross.
I don't want to go to bed,
NEVER wash my Super Ted.
Read me a story, but not too long,
Not that voice, you're reading it wrong.
Why do you get nothing right?
I love you Mum. Good night. Sleep tight.

Prompt 37: Pyramid

Write a poem which forms a pyramid on the page. It can have as many or as few lines as you like.

You might like to consider:

- How long should your poem be?

- Should you adhere to a strictly increasing number of words or syllables per line or write more freely governed by the appearance on the page?

- Could the appearance of your poem be relevant to its topic?

- Should you consider a double pyramid or other shape?

—— *Ups an Downs*

Life
Can feel
Hard to bear
And most unfair
An uphill struggle
And nightmarish muddle
You're fighting on your own.
But stop and look, and you will see
That though you're fully grown,
All around are helping hands,
Who'll guide and care and
Understand, as you find
Your way down. Let
Them help you,
Let them try
And never
Be afraid
To cry
X

Prompt 38: Forwards backwards

Write a poem which can be read either forwards or backwards (the last line, or stanza, becomes the first and so on).

You might like to consider:

- How can you use the reversal to make a point or tell a story?

- What should be your first and last lines?

- Should you try to make your poem tell the same or a different story when reversed?

- Should you make it clear to the reader that the poem can be read two ways?

—— *Adolescent Lament*

Why are we here
What does it mean
Does anyone care
If I keep my room clean
Does it matter a bit
If I shout and I spit
If I'm rude and unpleasant
Will someone notice it
I feel all alone
Nobody cares
Day after day
I'm fed up of their stares
I'm not normal they say
They all call me gay
It sucks being me
Day after day

Prompt 39: Climbing

Write a poem which includes climbing.

You might like to consider:

- Should you include literal or metaphorical climbing, or both?

- Who or what should be climbing and why?

- Should climbing form the central theme of your poem?

- Can you use rhyme, rhythm or the way the words are laid out on the page to add to the idea of climbing?

- Should you include climbing up and climbing down?

- Perhaps you should consider including falling?

—— Life's Ladder

The more we climb,
The further we'll fall,
Maybe we shouldn't
Climb at all?
From way up high,
The ground looks far,
But up here's
Where our life's dreams are.
So maybe it's worth,
The risk we run,
If we don't climb,
We'll have no fun.
And if we fall,
We could climb some more
A different route
Than we tried before.

Prompt 40: Heirloom

Write a poem which imagines the story behind an heirloom.

You might like to consider:

- Should you choose a family heirloom about which you know the story, or something else?

- Should you try to tell an accurate history or imagine a new past for the item?

- Who has used it, when, why? How did you come to know of it/own it or see it?

- What do you imagine its future holds?

—— To My Special Ring

I look at you and wonder,
About your former life;
When you once adorned the finger
Of another petite wife.
It's been quite a long time,
Since you last sat upon a finger,
My husband's great great grandmother,
Her memory still lingers,
As I look upon these diamonds
Of this dainty ring of mine,
Your husband had exquisite taste,
As, of course, does mine.
This ring marked your engagement,
A hundred years ago or more,
I think you had a happy life,
Despite living through the war.
I wonder where this ring has been,
What with you did it do?
Your fingers were so tiny that
It only fitted you.
So since you died some time ago,
It lived inside a box,
Getting old and dull and grey,
Behind Tom's mum's old frocks.
But you have a new life now,
I wear you every day,
And every time I look at you,
I feel a special way;
You remind me that Tom loves me,

You were a gift to mark ten years,
You remind me too of times gone by,
Of blood and sweat and tears,
Of those lives that went before our own,
But for us paved the way,
I know you're only jewellery,
But you make me smile each day.

Prompt 41: The wrong response

Write a poem which tells the story of a time you have given an inadequate or inappropriate response to something you've been told.

You might like to consider:

- When have you said the wrong thing?

- How did you feel afterwards?

- How did the other person respond?

- What could you have said that would have been more appropriate?

— Oh.

Oh.
The only word I found
To meet this dreadful news.
Oh.
I said as he revealed
A fate you'd never choose.
Oh.
My mind completely blank,
And reeling from the shock.
Oh.
I said, and then
I disappeared around the block.

Prompt 42: Loss of sense

Write a poem which explores how it might feel to lose one of your senses.
   You might like to consider:

- Which sense should you explore?
- Should you write in the first person or perhaps explore the experiences of someone you know?
- What emotions would come with this loss of sense?
- Which things would no longer be possible or would be very different?
- Would there be any positive aspects to a loss of a sense?
- Should you talk of a temporary or permanent loss?

—— Losing Sight

Her world grew darker every day,
Once vivid colors faded grey,
And with the darkness came dark moods,
Inspired by simple things like foods
She couldn't see, but had to eat,
Faceless nurses she must meet,
Shoes put on the wrong feet first,
The wrong juice slurped to quench her thirst.
She knew she should be brave and strong,
What sight she had would soon be gone.
Her loss of sight came not with grace,
Tears would trace lines down her face,
An artist in her younger days,
Her blindness left her in a maze
Devoid of colour, ugly, dark,
She dared not venture near a park,
For fear of sights that she would miss,
You should go! Her son would hiss.
Her son, to her, was faceless now,
She must go on. She knew not how.

Prompt 43: Stigma

Write a poem which explores stigma.

You might like to consider:

- What should be at the center of the stigma in your poem? Race, religion, mental health etc.?

- What perspective should you tell your poem from?

- Have you experienced or witnessed stigma?

- Why do people hold stigmatising views? How are these perpetuated?

- What impact do they have?

- How might they be changed?

—— Stop and Try My Shoes

Next time
You deign to look at me
With a hate filled heart,
Judgement
Clouding your eyes,
Stop,
For one moment,
And think:
If I looked at you,
With a heart full of hate,
And judging eyes.
How would you feel?
Step into my shoes,
And feel
How uncomfortable they are.
Remember those oozing blisters,

The next time our paths collide.

Prompt 44: Hope

Write a poem which aims to give hope to someone who has lost theirs.

You might like to consider:

- Is there someone in your life to whom you'd like to offer hope?

- How can we overcome a sense of hopelessness?

- Why is it important that we try?

- How different does life feel with hope than without it?

- How can you use rhyme or rhythm to portray hope?

- Could you play with rhyme or rhythm to portray a sense of hopelessness at the start building to a more upbeat, hopeful finish?

Harm and Hope

Everything felt too much,
He needed it to stop.
Huddled in the bathroom,
Locked away and shaking,
He had a choice to make.
He had a razor blade in one hand,
A picture of his brother in the other.
He turned the blade over in his hand.
It taunted him.
He knew its secrets;
The relief it would bring,
Followed by the ache of guilt.
Tempted by the thought of relief,
He pressed the razor to his skin,
But then he caught his brother's eye,
Looking up at him
With a shiny gloss finish
And a heart full of love.
I cannot do this with you watching…
He concluded.
He put the blade away,
Secreting the picture with it.
He had not placed the picture there.
He did not know his brother knew.
He had said nothing.
As he left the bathroom,
He passed his brother on the stairs.
His eyes passed over his brother's fading scars,

Criss-crossing strong black arms.
Thank you.
He muttered,
Knowing his brother would understand.
His brother always understood.
You can do this.
Said his brother,
You are stronger than me,
And between us,
We have the strength of three.
You can do this,
And I'll help you.

Prompt 45: Controversial

Write a poem which addresses a topic people usually choose not to talk about.
You might like to consider:

- What topic should you cover?

- Is the topic important to you? Why?

- Why don't people normally talk about it? How do they usually respond if it comes up?

- What do you hope to achieve with your poem? To start conversations? To break down stigma? To show your stance on a topic?

- Should you reel the reader in by only mentioning the taboo topic towards the end?

⸺ Light Extinguished

There was a light,
But the tunnel felt so long.
Keep trying…
People urged
You can do it…
They cat called half-heartedly,
Not really believing what they said.
But he didn't want to.
Why should he?
Could he not just give up?
What about your children…
The voices echoed
What about them…
He wondered.
Perhaps they'd be better off without him.
Perhaps he simply wasn't good enough.
Perhaps this was where it should end.
Here,
In this tunnel,
Dimly lit by a distant light.
He was dragged from the tunnel.
Kicking and screaming.
Given a second chance
That he desperately
Did.
Not.
Want.

Now he looks back on that time;
I always had hope.
He says.
I did it for the children.
He says.
I knew I had to keep trying.
He says.
And inwardly wonders
If he deserved to be saved.

Prompt 46: Happy sad

Write a poem which explores how it feels to put a brave face on things.
You might like to consider:

- Why do we pretend to be happy when we're sad?

- Does it help us to feel happier if we pretend to be?

- What would happen if we stopped pretending?

- How does it feel to harbour secret, sad, feelings?

—— *Fake Smile*

You want to reassure yourself,
I want to reassure you too,
So we're both complicit
In the smile I fake for you.
I know all the mechanics
Of just how a smile looks;
I've seen it on the internet,
Read about it in some books.
It feels all wrong upon my face
Like someone forced it there
But once you see my smile
You pass straight by without a care.
I'm quite relieved, I couldn't manage
'How are you's' today.
I know you know I'm faking,
But we're both content this way.

Prompt 47: Unlikely Haiku

Write a Haiku (see the section on *Poetic Forms* earlier in Part Three) which celebrates the beauty of something which is not generally considered beautiful.

You might like to consider:

- Should you choose something living or something inanimate?

- Is there something you find a hidden beauty in you can explain to others?

- Should you choose the least likely thing possible and perhaps make it funny?

- Should you write one Haiku or a series?

—— *Love is not heart-shaped*

> Love is not heart-shaped
> It is shaped like full sick bowls
> And vomity hugs

Prompt 48: Twenty-nine

Write a poem which contains exactly twenty-nine words

You might like to consider:

- How should you form your poem, e.g. how many words per line?

- Should you refer to the number twenty nine in your poem?

- What type of poem should you write – happy, sad, funny, reflective?

— *S.A.D.*

Caterpillar crawling,
Cherry blossom falling
Now the weather's warming
I feel fine.

When the weather's bleaker
It leaves me feeling weaker,
I certainly act meeker
But now I'm fine.

Prompt 49: Holding hands

Write a poem in which hands are held.

You might like to consider:

- Who is holding hands with who?

- Why?

- How does it make each of the people feel?

- How would they feel without the hand-holding?

— Hand Holding

I promise I will hold your hand,
In good times and in bad.
I'll hold it very tightly if
You're ever feeling sad.

I'll reach out for your manly paw
At times when you're excited,
And if we part I'll grab your hand
When we are reunited.

I'll hold your hand when tears flow
With grief, or joy, or sorrow,
And all the time your hand's in mine,
I'll welcome more tomorrows.

I hope there never comes a time,
When you won't hold my hand,
Whether we're out shopping
Or making footprints in the sand.

They say home is where the heart is,
And perhaps the saying's true,
But I also know I'm always home,
When holding hands with you.

Prompt 50: Random word

Write a poem which starts with a random word – generate your word by visiting this site: http://creativitygames.net/random-word-generator/randomwords or by opening a book at random and picking a word.

You might like to consider:

- What were your first thoughts upon seeing your word?

- Should your word dictate the central theme of your poem?

- If you're feeling brave, you could pick more than one random word to feature in your poem.

My random word was 'Gaggle'

—— *Happy Talk*

The evening drew in
And they talked and they talked
As the stars shone
They talked a bit more.
Who started,
Who finished,
And who said the most,
None of them could be quite sure.
But the thing that they knew
As the cold darkness grew,
Was that talking had done them some good.
And this gaggle of friends,
Felt happy and safe,
In the way the best happy friends should.

Final thoughts from Pooky

I hope you find the ideas and poems shared within this book a useful starting point for difficult conversations that might not otherwise have been had. Whilst I have tried to provide as many ways in as possible for you and the person you're supporting, I hope I haven't been overly prescriptive. Trust your instincts, be bold and adventurous in your use of poetry and feel free to think completely outside the boxes I have painted here. I have found poetry to be a powerful tool both personally and professionally; I hope you find it so too. Good luck on your journey and please be in touch with your poems or experiences of using poetry.

Pooky

Twitter: @PookyH

Email: pooky@inourhands.com

https://pookypoetry.wordpress.com – my daily poems

www.inourhands.com – my mental health resources and blog posts

Index of poems

Index of poetry prompts